Effective Group
Problem Solving

William M. Fox

Effective Group Problem Solving

*How to Broaden Participation,
Improve Decision Making, and
Increase Commitment to Action*

Jossey-Bass Publishers
San Francisco • Oxford • 1990

EFFECTIVE GROUP PROBLEM SOLVING
How to Broaden Participation, Improve Decision Making, and Increase Commitment to Action
by William M. Fox

Copyright © 1987 by: Jossey-Bass Inc., Publishers
350 Sansome Street
San Francisco, California 94104
&
Jossey-Bass Limited
Headington Hill Hall
Oxford OX3 0BW

Library of Congress Cataloging-in-Publication Data

Fox, William M.
Effective group problem solving.

(A Joint publication in the Jossey-Bass management series and the Jossey-Bass social and behavioral science series)
Bibliography: p. 181
Includes index.
1. Problem solving, Group.   I. Title.   II. Series: Jossey-Bass management series.   III. Series: Jossey-Bass social and behavioral science series.
HD30.29.F69   1987   658.4′036   86-33742
ISBN 1-55542-033-8

Manufactured in the United States of America

The paper in this book meets the guidelines for permanence and durability of the Committee on Production Guidelines for Book Longevity of the Council on Library Resources.

JACKET DESIGN BY WILLI BAUM

FIRST EDITION
First printing: March 1987
Second printing: February 1988
Third printing: August 1990

Code 8710

A joint publication in
The Jossey-Bass Management Series
and
The Jossey-Bass
Social and Behavioral Science Series

Contents

**Part Three: Strengthening Various Participation-Based
Approaches**

Preface

Effective Group Problem Solving describes what you can gain by using participative problem solving in your regular work group, committee, or volunteer group. It discusses the impressive achievements of participation-based programs in industry and elsewhere and provides fair warning to organizations about the disadvantages they may face if they fail to understand and learn from these programs. Of greater importance, it presents a process—the Improved Nominal Group Technique (INGT)—that consists of research-based rules and procedures that minimize or eliminate the many problems associated with conventional group procedures.

Challenge to Tradition

In America today we are witnessing a movement away from traditional authoritarian relationships toward high employee involvement in decision making. This movement was given a special boost at a White House conference on productivity in 1983. Most speakers strongly endorsed employee participation as an effective means for increasing productivity. Representatives of government, industry, and higher education pointed to various specialized groups, such as labor-management committees and quality circles, as being particularly useful (Guzzo, 1984).

This view echoes the findings of Peters and Waterman, who investigated excellence in America's leading firms. They reported that "excellent companies treat the rank and file as the root source of quality and productivity gain. They do not foster we/they labor attitudes" (1982, p. 14). And Lawrence and Dyer (1983) report the results of an in-depth study of the recent history of notable firms in seven basic U.S. industries (automobile manufacturers, steel, hospitals, agriculture, residential construction, coal, and telecom- .nunications) that have been confronted by dramatic changes in their operating environments. They conclude that "although organizations can get by for a time being only efficient or only innovative, over the long term there must be a simultaneous achievement of both efficiency and innovation. . . . Member involvement is essential to the simultaneous achievement of both efficiency and innovation" (p. 267).

Effective Group Problem Solving will reveal how improved group problem-solving procedures can contribute significantly to achieving high employee involvement, increasing productivity, and encouraging innovation.

In the larger community in which we live, both citizens and responsible officials have been frustrated by the inadequacies of conventional means for gathering and using informed public opinion on the social needs and complex problems confronting us. The kind of informed involvement that characterized our best town meetings of the past has become a casualty of modern, complex society. Today, large public meetings often succumb to dominant oratory, or degenerate into shouting matches, or simply flounder in the common frustration of many would-be contributors confronting too-little time. We are losing what Susan Mohrman (1979) calls *political access:* the ability to raise issues and the ability to seriously attend to those issues. This is a significant social problem because most people value having real opportunities to influence decision making when they want them more than participation in and of itself.

Effective Group Problem Solving will describe how viable, consultative democracy can be introduced and sustained in both the workplace and in the larger community. We will observe the paradox of anonymity strengthening democracy by enhancing our individuality and see how we can be more productive by understanding the limits of our objectivity and the specific measures we can take to compensate for these limits.

Overview of the Contents

Chapter One explains why we should encourage participative problem solving. Chapter Two details problems commonly associated with conventional approaches to encouraging participation, and Chapter Three presents the nine principles underlying the rules and procedures of INGT and the reasons for their importance.

The next seven chapters provide details concerning the implementation of these improved rules and procedures and explain how they relate to the following objectives: identifying and prioritizing problems, positions, or options; solving a particular problem (when no standard solution is available); and debugging or refining a written proposal or other document.

Chapters Four and Five deal with setting the stage for full participation. They explain the importance of anonymity, of defining purpose realistically, and of a permanent display record, and they describe how to save valuable meeting time by using important premeeting preparation.

Chapter Six discusses how a meeting should be conducted. It stresses the pitfalls of premature evaluation or criticism of ideas and the advantages of providing real opportunities for discussion. It shows how to keep discussions on track by controlling personal conflict and chronic time wasting, without undermining full participation. Chapter Seven presents several useful ways to handle voting.

Chapter Eight presents the special characteristics and uses of the document review meeting, which is designed for debugging or refining a written proposal or other document. Chapter Nine traces the steps involved in implementing successful community-wide or organization-wide program planning, including an explanation of how to meld the output of two or more groups. Chapter Ten provides a summary and review of the entire INGT process.

Chapter Eleven explores key problem areas of management by objectives programs and shows how INGT can be used to deal with them. Chapters Twelve and Thirteen show how to gain the greatest advantages for the problem-identification and problem-solving activities of autonomous work groups, employee-employer boards, quality circles, survey feedback meetings, bargaining teams, confrontation meeting committees, project teams, volunteer venture teams, job-redesign teams, and Scanlon, Rucker, Improshare, and multiple-management plan committees.

Chapter Fourteen on organization development lists the basic requirements for successful collaborative diagnosis and problem-solving efforts and shows how INGT uniquely satisfies these requirements. Chapter Fifteen shows how to apply INGT to enhance the effectiveness of audio, video, and computer teleconferences, and Chapter Sixteen explores two other areas that may benefit from the principles and procedures of INGT: international relations and one-on-one relationships.

The book concludes with suggestions for preparing to lead your first meeting and a test for checking your understanding of the key rules and procedures of INGT.

The procedures outlined in this book differ significantly from everyday practice. Some of them may seem strange at first, but each plays an important role, for reasons that will be explained. Most participants who have tried them like them and prefer them over their present procedures. Have your group try them out on a matter of importance without omitting or changing anything. I believe that the results will speak for themselves quite positively.

Acknowledgments

The important role that process plays in group problem solving was first brought home to me by Norman R. F. Maier. He was deeply interested in the constructive sharing of influence, and I was fortunate enough to be a student of his at the University of Michigan. Because of his influence, the topic of my doctoral dissertation was "An Experimental Study of Group Reaction to Two Types of Conference Leadership."

I have received invaluable assistance in developing this manuscript. Among those who have read it and then provided encouragement and many useful suggestions are Chris Argyris of Harvard University, Nancy Badore of Ford's Organization Development and Management Training Division, Alan Filley of the University of Wisconsin, Sud Ingle of Quality Circle Services, Tapas Sen of AT&T's Human Resources Division, and James Showkeir of TRW's training and development staff.

I am particularly indebted to Eric Trist, who has contributed so much to the quality of worklife worldwide, and to Richard Mason of Southern Methodist University for challenging me to make more of this undertaking than I otherwise would have and for pointing the way. I would also like to thank Marlene Baccala, who kept the word processor humming. Last, but in no way least, my wife, Else, has been a constant helpmate and an inspiration.

Gainesville, Florida   William M. Fox
January 1987

*For all problem-solving groups that aspire
to collaborate more equitably and more productively*

The Author

William M. Fox is a professor of management at the Graduate School of Business Administration of the University of Florida and a consultant. He received his B.B.A. and M.B.A. degrees in organizational behavior from the University of Michigan in 1948 and his Ph.D. degree in organization and management theory from Ohio State University in 1954.

    Fox has conducted leadership studies for the Office of Naval Research, studied Japanese management as a Senior Fulbright Research Scholar, and served as a management consultant to the air force. He has published several books and numerous articles. He is a member of the American Psychological Association and a Fellow in the Academy of Management.

Effective Group
Problem Solving

Chapter One

How Participation
Improves Problem Solving

Despite the many frustrations that go with conventional group problem solving, studies show that the benefits gained are usually worth the effort. Typically, several concerned and knowledgeable people will outperform one person in solving problems which do not have standard solutions.

Because it increases understanding and commitment, participation increases the likelihood of good solutions and of their effective implementation. Participation helps us to know the *whys* as well as the *whats* that are involved. It gives us a personal stake in what happens.

Other benefits of participation are enhanced team spirit, increased respect for an acceptance of the leader, and increased self-respect. We turn now to some concrete evidence.

People Want to Participate

Sirota (1969) surveyed IBM employees in forty-six countries about the type of supervision preferred. Consultation and joint decision making were clearly favored. Samuel (1972) obtained a similar result when he surveyed several hundred employees in nineteen organizations, representing six different industrial settings. Those surveyed indicated a practically uniform desire for greater participation, collaboration, and mutual responsiveness

1

than they were getting. Lawler, Renwick, and Bullock (1981) found that a group of 2,300 employees wanted significantly more influence over work-related decisions. A survey by IDE Research Group (1981) of 8,828 employees in 134 establishments in twelve countries found a desire for greater involvement in work-related decisions on the part of foremen and middle managers as well as workers.

Surveys show that a large group of priests and nurses also feel this way. A survey of 801 priests indicated that perceived influence in determining policies and actions was the most important factor associated with their satisfaction (Carey, 1972). Seventy-five percent of a group of 197 supervisory and nonsupervisory nurses, from all departments and levels in two urban hospitals, indicated that they felt deprived of participation on the job (Alutto and Vredenburgh, 1977).

These and other studies make it clear that there is an increasing demand on the part of better educated and rights conscious group members for a bigger role in defining, analyzing, and solving problems that concern them, both in the community and in the workplace. One survey, in particular, dramatizes this trend: the percentage of employees who rated their managements favorably dropped from 40 percent in 1975–79 to just over 20 percent in 1980–84 (O'Boyle, 1985). Undoubtedly, reluctance on the part of managers to share influence is a key reason for this decline. As Lawler observes: "People are becoming less comfortable with a society in which work organizations are autocratic while the political and other features of their lives are democratic" (1986, p. 19).

Participation Produces Better Results

On the average, several people will produce more and better solutions to a nonroutine problem than will a single person. This is the conclusion of a review of research studies which compare individual problem solving with conventional group problem solving (Shaw, 1976). Participation by group members facilitates understanding. Good solutions and challenging goals are valuable only to the extent that they are understood. Participation in goal setting and in problem solving increases our understanding of *what* is to be done and of *how* it is to be done (Latham and Saari, 1979).

Even when solutions or goals are well understood, they have limited value unless they are fully accepted. High commitment distinguishes superior performers from poor performers, highly satisfied performers from dissatisfied performers. Participation in group problem solving is one of the most effective means for gaining commitment. We have abundant research evidence to support this conclusion, as the following studies, conducted in a variety of work environments, demonstrate.

A Pajama Factory

Workers on an incentive piecework system were making pajamas for a market characterized by strong price competition and seasonal style changes. The company had a history of fair dealings, so it had enjoyed good labor relations since its founding.

The economic need for regularly changing the details of work and for shifting workers about was apparent to all. Yet, many workers reacted to change by quitting, or by taking more time than an average new employee needed to reach the standard rate, even though they had only to relearn at the average rate to receive a bonus.

Management decided to study different ways of dealing with change. Workers were divided into four groups matched in terms of skill level, amount of job change required, and degree of group cohesion or "we" feeling. Only minor changes in work and time standards were involved.

The hand pressers in group 1 were called together and told by the production manager why it was necessary to cut costs by simplifying the product, that sales would be lost if they could not match lower prices. The minor changes in work and the piecework rate were explained. Questions were invited and frank answers were given.

The pajama folders in group 2 were called together *before* any specific work changes had been decided upon, and the need for cost reduction was explained as done with group 1. Agreement was reached that necessary savings could be made through changes in the work; that representatives of the group would collaborate with management in determining the changes; and that these representatives would then master the new procedure, serve as time study subjects for setting a new rate, and assist in explaining the changes.

The pajama examiners in groups 3 and 4 were exposed to the same treatment as group 2, except that every member participated in planning and implementing the work changes. In view of the prestudy similarity of the groups and the relatively minor work changes made, the dissimilarities in their reactions are striking.

Members of group 1 rejected management's changes, despite the realistic explanations given and management's willingness to answer any questions. They regarded the changes as arbitrary and unreasonable. Their production dropped, from a prechange level of sixty units per hour to fifty units per hour, and it remained there until the group was broken up for reassignment thirty-two days after the change.

It was discovered later that the production drop resulted from group agreement to "get even" with management for its "unfair action." Three group members quit, there were strong expressions of aggression against management, and grievances were filed against the piece rate (which later study showed to be too generous rather than too "tight").

With dramatic contrast, production *rose* in the other three groups, from a prechange level of sixty units per hour, to seventy units per hour within thirty days after the change. No grievances were filed, no employees quit, and group members retained a cooperative attitude toward management. They referred to the changed job as "our job" and the changed rate as "our rate." In addition, the same supervisor who received criticism from group 1 received support and cooperation as the supervisor of group 2.

The main difference between group 2 (which had representatives participate) and groups 3 and 4 (which had all members participate) was the length of time that output stayed down after the work changes were made. The two full-participation groups recovered at a much faster rate.

There is an important postscript. Two-and-one-half months after their reassignment to other parts of the plant, the thirteen surviving members of group 1 were regrouped and assigned to a new presser job, one that presented about the same level of difficulty as the changed job they had refused to adjust to before the breakup of their group. This time, however, a full participation approach was used. The group's response now paralleled the positive responses that groups 3 and 4 had given to full participation (Coch and French, 1948; Marrow, Bowers, and Seashore, 1967).

What is striking about this study is the dramatic difference that participation made with regard to workers accepting changes which were logically in their best interests. After all, these workers were on an incentive pay system administered by trustworthy management, and all knew that their jobs would be threatened if the company became less competitive in a "dog-eat-dog" market.

Another study in the same pajama factory provides additional evidence about the value of group problem solving for obtaining acceptance of change. The director of personnel research wanted the management staff to accept the hiring of older people. The director had evidence to show that older people had the required skills and aptitudes, but the staff remained opposed. He suggested that the staff undertake a modest research project. Since older workers are inefficient, would it not be useful to determine the cost of continuing the older workers currently employed? They agreed, and undertook the study.

Results obtained by the management staff were contrary to their expectations, but similar to the research director's evidence, namely, that older people are desirable employees. This time, however, staff were willing to accept and act upon the evidence; now it was *their evidence* (Marrow and French, 1945).

A similar case for participation is made by Fleishman (1965). In a study of veteran workers in a positive work environment, representational involvement significantly reduced production drops that had previously accompanied changes in style instituted by management. Without input, worker dissatisfaction occurred despite the fact that each operator had continued to perform essentially the same basic operations.

An Aerospace Company

A large aerospace company, the primary supplier of electronics for ICBM guidance systems, experimented with participative management as a means of reducing errors and increasing employee satisfaction. Over a four-year period, some forty groups of employees became involved in a group problem-solving approach. In each case, the results indicate the importance of acceptance. For example, a group-set goal to reduce inspection paperwork errors by 50 percent produced a 75 percent reduction over a three-month period in one group; whereas, the same goal assigned individually in another group produced no change. A group of women requested and obtained music in their work area (via tapes and earphones) and their output increased significantly; however, when this same accommodation was extended unilaterally by management to other groups in the department, no changes in output occurred. Members of one of three groups doing assembly work requested that their work benches be turned around so that they could avoid facing a bare wall. Only the requesting group was noticeably pleased after management made the change for all three groups. The other two groups appeared indifferent.

Again, these results show how the way in which a change is made can have more influence on acceptance than the nature of the change itself. Over the four-year period, production increases averaged 20–30 percent and error reductions averaged 30–50 percent, in twenty-seven of the forty groups encouraged to participate in decision making (Hinrichs, 1978).

The Issue of Fairness

When an issue of fairness arises, what is viewed as being right usually depends upon the background and values of the viewer. Often, what a group leader would prescribe, even with the best of intentions, is not what his or her group would suggest. This difference has been demonstrated many times by running a study in which several groups are given the same "fairness" problem to solve.

One such problem might concern a foreman's assignment of a new truck to one of five drivers. It is not obvious who should get the truck. Each driver could make a claim, depending upon how one values such factors as seniority, amount of driving required, personal health, accident and maintenance records, preference about the make of truck, and the age and condition of each currently assigned truck.

Various groups have produced some thirty different solutions to this problem. They consistently prefer their own solutions, even after seeing the additional advantages offered by other solutions (BNA Films, 1965). In 76 percent of sixty-two groups in which leaders let the group decide, all group members were satisfied with the joint solution and only three percent of the groups had two or more dissatisfied members. However, in twenty-four groups in which the leader was perceived as dominating the decision process, only 4 percent of groups were free of dissatisfaction and 42 percent had two or more dissatisfied members (Maier and Hoffman, 1962). These results reinforce the fact that group member satisfaction can depend more upon an opportunity to participate—to "own" a solution—than upon the nature of the solution itself.

Scanlon, Rucker, and Improshare Plan Firms

Scanlon, Rucker, and Improshare plans provide employees with a form of partnership based on management's willingness to share productivity gains and influence. The success of this approach requires employee participation in problem solving. It offers the opportunity to challenge current ways of doing things, coupled with the responsibility for coming up with good alternatives. Problem identification and problem solving are accomplished in committees composed of both labor and management representatives. The importance of employee participation has been demonstrated repeatedly by the disappointing results associated with plans that have neglected this aspect (Fox, 1978; White, 1979).

The following results are attributed to adoption of the Scanlon plan by an electrical products company in Tennessee (G. Sherman's foreword to Moore and Ross, 1978):

- An average increase of 9 percent in direct labor efficiency;
- An increase of 16 percent in indirect or support labor productivity;
- Halving of the grievance rate;
- Reduction of the quit rate from an annual average of 30 percent to 5 percent; and
- Monthly employee bonuses averaging 13 percent of competitive base pay, in addition to greatly improved employee morale.

Of thirty successful Scanlon plan companies cited by Moore and Ross (1978), seven permitted the pooling of their financial data. They had paid an average monthly bonus of almost 10 percent above competitive base pay to their employees over a period of ten years.

Mitchell Fein (1982) reports an average 24.4 percent improvement in productivity for fifty-seven companies in their first year of using his Improshare plan. Workers were given 50 percent of the money saved.

The U.S. General Accounting Office (1981) made a study of twenty-four firms representing all three plans. It found that those in operation more than five years had averaged almost 29 percent labor cost savings for the most recent five-year period. Additional accomplishments commonly cited were better teamwork and cooperation, faster responses to problems, better product quality, less resistance to change, more employee involvement, and lower rates of absenteeism and turnover.

Salespeople

Traditionally, salespeople have been motivated by having their own territories, being on commission, and being encouraged to outdo each other. Research shows that a group problem-solving approach can produce even better results than this traditional approach.

In one study, a new regional sales manager held regular problem-solving meetings with his group of fourteen local sales managers. In turn, he encouraged them to hold such meetings with their salespeople. His region had been below the top one-fourth of all regions in performance at the time he took over. Within two years, it became the leading division and went on to improve that lead (Likert, 1961, pp. 188–190).

In another study, a consultant used attitude survey data to guide a regional sales manager and his subordinate managers toward a more supportive, group problem-solving approach to leadership. A significant shift in supervisory behavior in the desired direction was shown by a comparison of before and after data supplied by subordinate managers seven months later. Sales had risen from an average level to a point where they were higher than the sales of a larger region which had a 25 percent higher sales growth potential, and this increase in productivity was accompanied by increases in cooperation and teamwork at all levels (Likert and Likert, 1976, pp. 78–82).

Merchant Marine

Based on long-standing tradition and irrespective of nationality, merchant ship captains and their staffs have maintained social distance from their crews in that they have unilaterally made decisions about the running of their ships. They have created and maintained authoritarian shipboard cultures, nurtured by separate sleeping, dining, and recreational facilities.

Due to the growing contrast between these practices and a trend toward employee participation in industry, Norwegian shipping firms began in the 1960s to have difficulty in recruiting sailors for their ships. Consequently, in 1968, the planning of a program of research and development to improve the quality of working life in the merchant marine was undertaken by a group of researchers in collaboration with representatives from the unions, the industry, and the government. They decided to make and study significant changes in living arrangements, the organization of work, and the sharing of influence on two project ships (Thorsrud, 1981).

These changes were so productive that, over a six-year period, they were introduced on most of the forty-five ships of the firm that owned the two project ships, as well as to many ships of other firms. The Norwegian government initiated significant changes in the training of seamen, their career planning, and the design of merchant ships. And now, "Ship-Meets-Ship" conferences are held periodically so that representatives of different innovative ships can compare notes and enrich each other's practices.

According to Thorsrud, a key aspect of the program is that " . . . sailors were accepted as competent partners with a right to influence their future work environment" (1981, p. 323).

Salaried Retail Sales Clerks

Four department stores from a family-owned chain participated in this study. All four handled the same type of merchandise and utilized the same organization structure and operating procedures. Three were located in large, suburban shopping malls and one was located in a commercialized business district. No sales clerks were paid on a commission basis; however, a computerized record of each clerk's sales per hour was kept. Since surveys had revealed employee dissatisfaction with pay and various policies, management agreed to experiment with the following approaches in three of the four stores, using one (store A) as a control site:

Incentive Only Condition (store B). Sales goals were assigned to each department in store B, based on the previous year's level and on acceptability to the sales clerks. Those who performed best against these goals for the four-week period could choose from a list of incentives (established on the basis of a poll), such as a day off with pay, an outfit at cost, being assistant manager for a day, movie tickets, or being permitted to schedule one's hours of work.

Participation Only Condition (store C). Sales clerks were divided into discussion groups to determine the procedure that would be used for approaching customers during the four-week period. (A survey had indicated considerable resentment of management's required procedure.)

Combined Condition (store D). Sales clerks employed both the incentive condition of store B and the participation condition of store C. The procedure decided on for approaching customers was the same as that chosen by the sales clerks of store C.

The results were clear-cut. The sales clerks in store D, using both participation and incentives, sold significantly more per hour than the clerks in the other three stores. Neither store B nor store C sales clerks did significantly better than the clerks in store A, the control site.

When the four-week experimental treatments ended, the stores returned to their preexperiment sales levels. Six weeks after this, store A clerks were given the same incentive/participation treatment that store D clerks had received, with all three other stores serving as control sites. This time, store A clerks sold significantly more than all the other clerks (Neider, 1980).

In one respect, a similar result was obtained from the analysis of six years of data from the principal foundry of a medium size U.S. manufacturer. Workers participated in meetings to define and solve work-related problems, and received productivity bonuses in those weeks in which production costs fell below standard performance costs. Participation and financial incentive, employed together, produced a significantly bigger impact on productivity than either alone.

However, unlike the weaker treatments with the sales clerks, the more powerful forms of participation and monetary incentive used in the foundry *each* made a significant impact on output, participation being the more important of the two (Rosenberg and Rosenstein, 1980).

When we compare these results to those obtained in studying Scanlon, Rucker, and Improshare plan workers and sales personnel, we see a consistent trend: participation enhances the motivational effects of other incentives.

A Hospital

In a study by Bragg and Andrews (1973), a highly effective hospital laundry supervisor, who used a driving, authoritarian style of leadership, agreed to try a participative, decision-making approach with his group of thirty-two workers. The primary reason for the trial was to see if the work could be made more interesting, since the productivity of the group was already excellent.

Group meetings were called when there were specific proposals to discuss. Any aspect of managing the laundry could be considered at these meetings, except for union matters and personal grievances. This policy produced twenty-eight meetings in which 147 employee suggestions were discussed during the first fifteen months of the program.

Initial employee uncertainty about this new opportunity for participation gave way within two months to a positive attitude, which increased in strength thereafter. For example, in the thirty-eight reporting periods after the change, the rate of absenteeism for the group was lower than the overall hospital rate thirty-two out of thirty-eight times; whereas, before the change it had been lower only twenty-three out of thirty-eight times. Productivity rose from a prechange average of fifty pounds of laundry processed per paid employee hour (higher than output in two comparison hospitals) to seventy-eight pounds one year after the change. Productivity later stabilized at seventy-three pounds.

At the time this study was reported, the participation program had survived for three years and was still going strong. The laundry supervisor indicated that it would be easy for him to revert to his old style, but he would miss the satisfaction he had gotten from the participative approach. He added that he had not had to reprimand a single individual since making the change.

The increase in productivity is particularly impressive when we consider that output before the change was already excellent, and there was no monetary incentive involved. This success resulted in the introduction of participative decision making to the hospital's staff and to a medical records section, with beneficial results in both instances.

A Volunteer Organization

The relationship between leadership and organizational effectiveness was studied in a random sample of 104 local leagues of the League of Women Voters. Effectiveness was defined as the extent to which a league accomplished its goals. This was assessed by twenty-nine judges with broad league experience. They took into account the resources available to each league. Results showed that

- The greater the pressure to participate (from themselves, their fellow group members, and their discussion leaders), the more effective the league.
- The more a member saw a responsive interest in her ideas, the more likely she would be active.
- The presidents of the more effective leagues were seen as understanding the views and sentiments of members better than the presidents of the less effective leagues.

As in the preceding studies, an underlying theme is one of shared influence. League members associate the interest shown in their ideas with the amount of influence they feel they can exert (Likert, 1961). The more they feel that their participation is welcome and matters, the more committed they become to league activities.

This relationship between participation in decision making and attitudes toward involvement, motivation, and identification with an organization also held true for a large sample of industrial employees, specifically, 2,100 workers and 380 managers in various Scanlon plan companies (Frost, Wakeley, and Ruh, 1974).

In Conclusion

Research results provide a clear answer to the question: "Why invite participation?" Group problem solving gives us a better grasp of the problems we face, more and better solutions to them, and better commitment to making the solutions work in practice. These benefits, in turn, are associated with the ultimate payoffs of improved satisfaction and performance.

We have looked at only a part of the supporting evidence. A 1975 survey of fifty-seven field studies by the National Science Foundation found productivity increases due to worker participation in 80 percent of organizations studied, and a review of 103 worker productivity experiments by Katzell in 1977 confirmed this finding (Stokes, 1978–79). Additional evidence relevant to the performance of special types of participation groups is presented in Chapters Eleven through Thirteen.

However, a word of caution is in order. Some of the studies reviewed in this chapter involved participative group process in a larger organizational setting, with results reported in terms of organizational outcomes. Although effective group process is essential for successful participative management of an organization, there are other requirements as well. Foremost among these are an organizational climate that supports the sharing of influence and safeguards that protect all organization members from being penalized as a result of gains in effectiveness made possible by their problem-solving contributions.

Typically, managers associate increased output with good bonuses and increased job security; whereas, rank-and-file workers often associate it with reduced workweeks, unexplained job shifts, or termination. At the same time, many supervisors and staff specialists end up finding themselves "rewarded" for helping to create successful self-managing groups by having their responsibilities diminished and their futures made less certain.

Although the subject of this book—effective group problem solving—is a key requirement for overall organizational viability, it is but one of many factors. Lawler (1986) ably discusses the other requirements in his book, *High Involvement Management.*

Chapter Two

Shortcomings of Conventional Procedures in Gaining Participation

The gains made by participation through conventional procedures (documented in Chapter One) are particularly impressive when we consider the frustrations and costs that conventional procedures impose upon us. We will now examine these limitations in detail, so that we can more fully appreciate the need for, and the potential savings that can be realized from, the research-based, field-tested approaches presented in this book.

Procedural Problems

Inviting a free-for-all is obviously not the way to run a meeting. It is just as important to coordinate group problem-solving activity as it is any other kind of work activity, but how can this be done without straitjacketing creative effort?

The problem is bigger for the new chairperson or supervisor who must put a group to work before having time to be accepted. He or she can take charge right away and be damned for "acting like a boss," or she or he can get into bigger trouble by asking: "Any ideas about how we should proceed?" Often, rather than productive participation, the response will be indifference, confusion, or open competition for the leadership role.

What we want, of course, is the kind of group climate that will bring forth *all* useful ideas without creating anarchy and without wasting time. We want final decisions based on honest and informed assessment of all choices. But these things are much easier said than done, as demonstrated when the following well established procedures are attempted.

First Come, First Served. With this widely used procedure, meeting time and attention are allocated on the basis of the order in which individuals get the floor. Ideas are discussed as they come up, one at a time, until one is acceptable to the group. Common courtesy demands a certain degree of indulgence, whether or not the idea being presented is a good one.

Even if the group puts off making a final decision until everyone has had a chance to speak up, those who come last are often rushed. In fact, the group may spend so much time on the ideas first presented that better ones are not even heard.

Clearly, it makes more sense to begin by identifying all useful ideas, and then allocate group time and attention to them on the basis of their relative value. The chapters that follow will explain how to do this, while assuring equal opportunity for participation at the same time.

Parliamentary Procedure. As the size of a group increases beyond ten to fifteen members, threats of information overload and disorderly process grow. One solution is to be more formal and use parliamentary procedure. However, outside of the large legislative bodies for which it was designed, parliamentary procedure often creates more problems than it solves.

It uses a first come, first served approach, so we still have the problems discussed above. In addition, we face some new ones. A seconded motion can force people to evaluate and accept or reject a position before they are ready. They cannot evaluate the position relative to *all* useful possibilities. And, those who politely wait for the "right" time to present their ideas often find themselves out of luck.

Consequently, the climate created by parliamentary procedure is more suggestive of "You should pass this unless you can find serious fault with it" than of "Let us search for the best solution we can find." When balloting is public, a proposal's sponsor often looks around to see how people are voting, clearly implying that "a vote against my proposal is a vote against me."

With parliamentary procedure, a well-organized minority can impose its will on a group by exploiting what is called the *bandwagon effect*. Several members, by prior arrangement, make a quick succession of positive statements in support of a desired motion. Then, they call for a vote.

One study shows that the first proposal that gets fifteen more positive than negative comments is adopted 85 percent of the time, regardless of its quality; and, that when a higher quality solution is presented later in the meeting, it has little chance of replacing the poorer one (Maier, 1967).

In line with these observations, a study of the use of parliamentary procedure by a number of groups found that most of the time it did *not* facilitate movement toward genuine consensus (Guetzkow and Gyr, 1954).

"There must be a better way," we think. Fortunately, there is. This book shows how to avoid these problems while maintaining productive control, with a single group or multiple groups of up to twenty members each.

Subversive Influences

Even when we have better conventional procedures, we can be left with difficulties at the interpersonal level, as the following examples demonstrate.

Hidden Agenda. Participants are driven by needs and purposes which have little to do with the business at hand. Compulsive talkers, for instance, waste group time outrageously, yet, we usually do not want to be or cannot afford to be rude to them. Hostile individuals produce conflict by promoting themselves at the expense of others, as when masters of the put down make others look bad or appear wrong. Whatever the technique, they create a climate of intimidation that plays havoc with productive participation. Still others come with closed minds and an overriding need to defend their turf from real or imagined threats. They try to sandbag progress by raising procedural technicalities; or, they refuse to participate, later claiming that they were denied a fair chance to present their objections.

Status over Quality. When there are important status differences among group members, the quality of an idea often plays second fiddle. This is illustrated by a study in which sixty-two permanent aircraft crews were presented with a test problem. Only 6 percent of the higher status pilots failed to obtain crew acceptance of their solutions; whereas, 20 percent of the lower status navigators failed. This, despite the fact that 50 percent of the navigators had the correct solution in comparison to only 31 percent of the pilots (Torrance, 1955).

In another study, seventy five-member groups used conventional discussion procedures to deal with a common problem of judgment. The average group did not include the best ideas of its members in its final solution. Rather, subgroups formed to "sell" the rightness of a given solution, and individual dominance was quite evident (Tuckman and Lorge, 1962).

As a result of being largely ignored, lower status group members learn to withhold contributions with a "What's the use?" attitude. A survey of numerous discussion group studies bears this out. Unless lower status members are protected and encouraged, they will hold back (Hare, 1976). An additional problem, of course, is that the ignored lower status members are not likely to give their enthusiastic support to the group's decisions.

Even when we have status in the group, we may be reluctant to contribute if more able and experienced experts are present, not wanting to appear presumptuous. On the other hand, if we happen to be the most knowledgeable members present, we may withhold useful contributions to avoid the risk of monopolizing group time. Whatever the case, a group often ends up with a decision that is inferior to what it could have produced, had these restraints been eliminated or minimized.

Maintaining Control. Group leaders may believe that the only hope for avoiding loss of control of a meeting is to maintain a tight, personal rein on everything that happens. Their credo becomes "Give them an inch, and things will start to get out of hand." Unfortunately, more times than not, this will effectively prevent anything of value from happening. In addition, it may cause group members to view a leader as autocratic and egocentric.

Leader apprehension about losing control increases when group members represent competing groups or organizational units. It increases, also, when group members are able individuals from highly diverse backgrounds and the group has not yet reached a mature state of development. Under these conditions, there is a tendency for interpersonal competition to displace objective problem solving.

Conventional procedures do not facilitate dealing with such situations in a relaxed and constructive way. Their failure to provide an adequate impersonal basis for control may nudge a group leader toward undue reliance on personal status or formal position. The result is, despite the best intentions, we fail to realize the richness of group outcomes that a collection of able individuals has the potential to deliver. Unfortunately, after repeated failure to tap this potential, we may give up on the idea by forming safer, more homogeneous groups which have admittedly less problem-solving power.

Absenteeism and Tardiness. "Sorry I'm late," or "Wish I could have made the last meeting," the group member says. "Please fill me in on what has happened."

This is a tough request to deal with, especially if it comes from a key participant. It is easy to report any decisions that have been made, but how can we replay the thinking behind them without postponing or unduly delaying the present meeting? Yet, if we do not, the person's ability to contribute will be seriously handicapped.

Fear. Of all the factors that undermine productive participation, fear is probably the most common and may exist in many forms: fear of being punished for opposing the ideas of a boss or other powerful person; fear of hurting someone's feelings; fear of being embarrassed for putting forth what others may see as a foolish or questionable idea; or fear of rejection by the group for not sounding like a loyal "team player."

Apparently, such fears played a key part in the planning fiascoes behind the Bay of Pigs invasion and the escalation of the war in Vietnam. The President's chief advisers were perceptive and experienced individuals; but, collectively, they failed to deal with many dangers and uncertainties (Janis, 1972).

Furthermore, escalating commitment to a questionable course of action can be further strengthened when a leader manipulates data, such as focusing upon vivid anecdotal information rather than objective facts (Schwenk, 1986).

The procedures presented in this book show how to avoid or minimize the kinds of subversive influences we have discussed. They make it possible to establish and maintain effective control on an impersonal, noninhibitive basis. Their use eliminates uncertainty about whether or not a collaborative, creative process will be permitted to occur. In addition, their use in a group problem-solving setting fosters the view of the leader as a facilitator rather than boss.

Outside Experts

Can we increase the likelihood that the use of an outside consultant will be cost effective? A consultant often requires many days of study, at a high fee per day plus expenses, before he or she knows enough about a situation to be able to make useful contributions. Is there some way to reduce this cost without reducing the consultant's value to us?

How can we create a climate in which a consultant's useful ideas will be accepted and inappropriate ones rejected by our staff without alienating the consultant?

Given the resentment of insiders toward a NIH (Not Invented Here) idea, the influence of status on idea evaluation, and a consultant's need to save face, the requirements discussed above are difficult to satisfy. This book presents effective means for satisfying them.

Time Constraints

Participation can consume too much time. Think of the factors we have discussed:

- The first come, first served approach;
- Compulsive talkers;
- Pursuit of personal objectives on group time;
- Time required to brief absentees and latecomers;
- People beating around the bush, afraid to tell it like it is; and
- Time required to brief consultants.

Is it any wonder that we find ourselves saying: "Sure, we'd like to have our people review all of our rules, policies, and procedures on a regular basis," and "Yes, we'd like to permit fuller participation in the meetings we have," but "Have you any idea of the amount of time that would be required? We just don't have it."

How many meetings start out on a participative note only to end on an autocratic one because time runs out? How discouraging it is to observe the railroading of poorly considered decisions at the end of a meeting. We think: "Is this the best we can do? There must be a better way." Well, there is. This book shows how to get more mileage out of meeting time than you may have thought possible, *without* scrimping on the quality of participation.

In Conclusion

The benefits of participation (demonstrated in Chapter One) are supported by theorists who point up the need for an organization to maintain a balanced combination of the following six pairs of properties if it is to be adaptive: (1) consensus and dissension; (2) contentment and dissatisfaction; (3) affluence and poverty; (4) planning and spontaneity; (5) change and stability; and (6) rationality and wisdom (Hedberg, Nystrom, and Starbuck, 1976).

Effective participation at work is essential to most of these ends. It helps to identify key problems, solve them, and make the solutions work more effectively. It enhances team spirit, respect for the leader, and our own self-respect.

In addition, it appears to have important implications for our ability to function as productive citizens. Karasek (1981) tracked workers over a period of years and found that those whose jobs had become less demanding, with diminished control over job-related decisions, had become more passive in their leisure and political participation; whereas, those whose jobs had become more demanding, with increased control over job-related decisions, had become more active in their leisure and political participation. Thus, he found a clear link between participation at work and enhanced community activity.

Still, the many headaches we have reviewed in this chapter remain. As an eminent researcher/consultant points out: "My experience is that only a few managers who have grown up with traditional approaches to management can change to be effective in participative systems. There simply seems to be too much to unlearn and too many roadblocks to new learning" (Lawler, 1984, p. 324).

Conventional problem-solving procedures exact a high price in time, frustration, and inefficiency. This book resolves the dilemma. It shows how to lower the price, while improving the benefits.

Chapter Three

Designing an Improved Approach: Nine Proven Principles for Effective Participation

We will now examine each of the nine guiding principles for effective participation in problem-solving groups that underlie the Improved Nominal Group Technique (INGT) presented in this book. When these principles are satisfied, through implementation of the rules and procedures presented in Chapters Four through Nine (and summarized in Chapter Ten), the many problems associated with conventional group problem-solving procedures will be eliminated or minimized.

First Principle: Assure Anonymity of Input Authorship

We try to please those in our work situation who control the things we need and want. They aren't always right, but they are almost always in a position of advantage relative to us. We try to avoid disagreeing with them, criticizing their actions, and in any other way offending them. And we don't forget this need to play it safe when we enter a problem-solving meeting.

When we become leaders, however, we often forget about this form of self-imposed censorship. We may become like the manager in the cartoon who tells his subordinates to give honest opinions, even if it costs them their jobs. We expect to get frank and unrestrained input, simply by asking for it. We assume too readily that when they are silent, group members either have nothing to say or agree with what is being said. After all, we reason, should not mature, competent adults be expected to speak up when they need to? Chapter Two explained why these are poor assumptions.

Improved Input. What we *think* are the most important problems for others may be an unwarranted projection of our own concerns. This is illustrated by a study involving twenty-three executives who represented different functions in the same organization. They were asked to identify, prior to specific discussion, what they considered to be the most important problem in a standard business case from the viewpoint of the top executive's position. Each executive tended to pick that aspect of the case which related to her or his particular areas of training and experience (Dearborn and Simon, 1958).

On the other hand, we may be fooled by what we hear in meetings from people who are wary of making their true feelings known. This was illustrated by Sullivan's (1978) study with university ROTC cadets. For the topic, "How can the operation of the local ROTC unit be improved upon?" he obtained more and better ideas from groups which gave input anonymously than from groups which made their input public. As we would expect, few cadets wanted to be identified as critics of the officers and noncommissioned officers who would influence their military futures.

The value of identifying problems anonymously is also shown by a study revealing the discrepancy between how supervisors describe their own behavior in dealing with their subordinates and how their subordinates describe it when permitted to do so anonymously.

One question asked how the supervisor gave recognition for good work. Note in Table 1, below, the difference between supervisor and subordinate use of the *very often* response.

Additional evidence was obtained from a multinational sample of 178 managers and their subordinates. Seventy-one percent of the managers saw themselves as using a "consulting"

Table 1. Self-Evaluation vs. Anonymous Input.

Recognition for Good Work	Supervisors Say "Very Often"	Subordinates Say "Very Often"
Gives privileges	52%	14%
Gives more responsibility	48%	10%
Gives a pat on the back	82%	13%
Gives sincere and thorough praise	80%	14%
Trains for better jobs	64%	9%
Gives more interesting work	51%	5%

Source: Based on research by Mann and Dent, 1954; adapted from the presentation in Likert, R. *New Patterns of Management.* New York: McGraw-Hill, 1961, p. 91. Used by permission.

style of leadership; whereas, only 29 percent of their subordinates agreed with this description (Sadler and Hofstede, 1972). Other researchers report the same findings (Argyris, 1966; "A Methodology for Participative Formulation . . . ," 1979).

Perhaps the members of your group have really leveled with you. Perhaps you know their feelings and concerns accurately. But why risk serious errors and oversights? There is much to gain from anonymous inputting and nothing to lose.

Effective Leadership. Leaders who want group member participation in problem solving face two problems: (1) how to get leader contributions evaluated on the basis of merit rather than source; and (2) how to make contributions without discouraging full participation on the part of others.

A leader can *tell* group members to forget his or her special status as leader, but this is unrealistic; and listeners may feel that it indicates naivete or untrustworthiness. Research results clearly show that, despite such instructions, a contributor's status has more influence on group decisions than the quality of his or her ideas.

In the Torrance (1955) study discussed in Chapter Two, we saw how higher status pilots were much more successful in getting their solutions accepted than were lower status navigators, even though 50 percent of the navigators had the correct solution, compared to only 31 percent of the pilots.

Another study makes the point more dramatically. In response to a high-status researcher, various subjects gave what they thought were increasingly stronger electric shocks to actors, who pretended to experience greater pain with each "jolt." A majority of subjects clearly did not want to give the shocks. Many protested; some broke out in a cold sweat. But, most did what the influential researcher told them to do (Milgram, 1965).

The second problem that leaders face is that of their own contributions discouraging other contributions—a problem very real to group members, although leaders tend to overlook it. The leader makes a proposal. We feel obligated to discuss it before looking at other ideas, often devoting more time than we should. Then, being unable to reject it, we feel pressured into voting its acceptance, thereby slamming the door on other possibilities.

We leave such a meeting with the feeling that we have been exploited. We wonder if the leader really thinks that a genuine group decision was produced, or if he or she wants it this way, with only lip service being paid to participation.

Yet, a leader should not be limited to the role of directing group process. Typically, a leader has important contributions to make. The question is "How can we have *both* leader contribution and good leadership at the same time?"

The solution is anonymous inputting. Most of the time, a leader can present his or her ideas in a form that will not disclose authorship. Then, these ideas can be evaluated and acted on on the basis of their merit. Janis (1972), originator of the term *group-think,* stressed this need for a leader to conceal preferred positions at the beginning of a meeting in order to create a climate that encourages participants to express doubts and counterarguments.

Since the procedures in this book do not follow a first come, first served rule, the leader and other participants can make an unlimited number of anonymous contributions without monopolizing group time or attention.

Utilization of Newcomers. Most consultants are cautious about sticking their necks out. They know they will succeed only to the extent that their ideas fit local conditions. Consequently, they can consume surprising amounts of study and briefing time, at client expense, in preparing to contribute.

Other outsiders may offer ideas prematurely. Knowing they mean well, insiders often spend a disproportionate amount of time in trying to reject their ideas tactfully. This problem can be particularly acute for a program planning task force made up of representatives from different agencies.

New supervisors who do not know the local ropes can really get into trouble. They may not be able to put off committing themselves, as do the consultants, and they usually stand to lose more through inappropriate inputting than do other participants.

The solution to all three of these newcomer situations lies in anonymous inputting. Ideas flow freely. They may be adapted to the group's needs, or they may be easily rejected. The need to save face is minimized.

Satisfaction and Motivation. In addition to making problem-identification and problem-solving meetings more productive, assured anonymity increases the likelihood that the value of individual contributions will be fairly recognized. The importance of this is underscored by a comprehensive study at a large national chain of retail stores.

Researchers found that the satisfaction and motivation of both employees and managers were significantly affected by whether or not they felt their contributions were recognized. As Figures 1 and 2 show, those who responded favorably to the question of recognition felt much better toward their work, supervisors, organizations, and careers than those who said their contributions were not recognized. Furthermore, these findings were found to apply across a wide spectrum of occupational groups in the company (Smith, 1972).

Able group members with low status have a special need for anonymous inputting. Without it, their contributions encounter indifference and unfair criticism and are thereby less likely to receive fair recognition. These members soon give up on trying to contribute, and their resulting silence and voting conformity are misread as agreement. Later, they may retaliate by withholding their support from the effective implementation of the decisions

Figure 1. Morale Index: Technical Specialists.

	Degree of Employee Satisfaction and Motivation				
	Low	Moderately Low	Neutral	Moderately High	High
Supervision	Yes (Contribution Recognized)				
	No				
Kind of Work					
Amount of Work					
Financial Rewards					
Career Future and Security					
Company Identification					

Source: Adapted from Smith, 1972. Used by permission.

made. This damaging process is well documented by research findings (Torrance, 1957; Hare, 1976).

Use of Power. Actions speak louder than words. Support for the routine use of anonymous inputting helps a leader to establish and maintain her or his trustworthiness about using power responsibly. It clearly communicates: "I want to know what you're really thinking, I don't want to play games."

In this regard, a study of 250 teachers in seventeen elementary schools is of interest. The results indicate that it is "the ability to raise issues and meet with others in the system to aggregate views that results in a sense of trust that decisions in the organization take one's interests and views into account" (Mohr-

Figure 2. Morale Index: Merchandise Executives.

	Degree of Employee Satisfaction and Motivation				
	Low	Moderately Low	Neutral	Moderately High	High
Supervision	Yes (Contribution Recognized) No				
Kind of Work					
Amount of Work					
Financial Rewards					
Career Future and Security					
Company Identification					

Source: Adapted from Smith, 1972. Used by permission.

man, 1979, p. 203). And such trust was strongly related to perceived organizational effectiveness.

Second Principle: Define Purpose Realistically

The hardest meeting to conduct well is one with a combination of nonroutine purposes, especially when working against a time limit. As time runs out with much business left unfinished, we face a growing pressure to get on with it. Meaningful participation gets shortchanged, but we reason that, at least, we have saved time. However, if we count the time subsequently required to deal with misconceptions and nonacceptance, it is a costly illusion.

We have a tendency to seek solutions prematurely. We need to give adequate attention to identifying and defining problems before we try to solve them. Research results show that it pays to devote sufficient time and effort to *both* the "problem-mindedness" and "solution-mindedness" phases of group process (Van de Ven and Delbecq, 1971). Consequently, whenever possible in a given meeting, we should deal with just *one* of the following purposes: (1) identifying and prioritizing problems, positions, or options; (2) solving a particular problem; or (3) debugging or refining a written proposal or other document.

Document Review Meeting. Some problems should be assigned to a special task force due to their complexity and so that problem-solving activity can be coordinated with library and survey research when necessary. Afterward, all who have a stake in the matter can meet in a *document review meeting*, to consider the task force's written report, which should be distributed in advance of the meeting.

Nutt (1976, 1977) describes circumstances in which this approach can avoid needless difficulties. He shows that consumers of home health care services are better qualified to identify new opportunities and problems they encounter than to effectively resolve them into integrated delivery systems. On the other hand, the professional providers of such services are better qualified to formulate optimal delivery systems, given appropriate system objectives.

We can invite difficulties needlessly when we assign *both* the identification of the problems/opportunities phase and the solution phase of activity to a mixed group of consumers, professional providers, and other concerned parties. Given their stake in existing systems and relationships, many professional providers will try to dampen the innovative and critical thrusts of the more consumer-oriented activity of identifying problems and opportunities. Conversely, few nonprofessionals have much to contribute to the technical aspects of systems design once system objectives are agreed on.

The following process helps to avoid such problems:

1. Hold problem-identification meetings for nonprofessionals to identify and prioritize problems and opportunities.

2. Hold objectives-identification meetings of nonprofessionals and professionals together to finalize system objectives. (Any absolute constraints that must be satisfied should be communicated to participants before the meeting.)
3. Have professionals develop detailed system design plans for meeting the identified objectives.
4. Submit plans to a document review meeting, involving the same participants as in step 2 with the topic, "How can we improve on these plans?"

Other occasions that warrant a document review meeting include:

•   A supervisor wants his or her group to review a proposed budget or a plan handed down from above, or one that she or he has developed.
•   The need arises to review an interagency proposal developed by representatives of several groups.
•   The time comes for a periodic review of existing rules, policies, and procedures to see if they are still appropriate or can be improved upon.

An easy alternative, of course, is to pass out such materials for private, individual review. But there are good reasons why we should not settle for this:

•   We are more likely to produce superior proposals when we know they are going to be reviewed in a special meeting.
•   We are more likely to find bugs and come up with improvements when we are stimulated by each other's thinking.
•   We are more likely to achieve active participation of *all* stakeholders in such a meeting, and this will produce improved understanding and acceptance of the finished product.

Constraints and Opportunities. An option-identification, problem-solving, or document review meeting will be handicapped if participants do not have advance knowledge of special constraints—whether financial, technical, ethical, political, or legal—that must be satisfied. Participants may be aware of constraints; but it is good practice to list them in the announcement of the meeting just to be sure.

If there is doubt about any of them, and the answer cannot be found in existing sources, we should call a problem-solving meeting to determine the answers; or, ask a committee or an expert individual to write up proposed conditions for consideration in a document review meeting.

In addition, it may be useful to communicate in advance any characteristics that will enhance the value of an option, solution, or change if these are not apparent. For example, participants may know that we must reduce order-processing time by six days, but they may not realize that additional time reductions will be worth so much per day.

Third Principle: Collect and Distribute Inputs Before the Meeting

We draw on the innovative Delphi technique (Dalkey and Helmer, 1963) for valuable premeeting activity. It is a proven procedure that allows us to obtain many inputs, and lets participants see them and think about them in advance of the problem-solving meeting. We build on our collective thinking *before* we actually meet. There are several advantages.

First, required meeting time is reduced. Most of us can relate to the question: "Why spend meeting time on things we can do as well or better on our own?" This question has special meaning for executives. A six-day observation of three presidents of small companies revealed that they spent 21 percent of their time in scheduled meetings. A twenty-five-day observation of five chief executives of large companies turned up a figure of 59 percent, and a survey of 210 civilian executives in the public sector produced a figure of 45 percent (Mintzberg, 1973; Lau, Newman, and Broedling, 1980).

When anonymous premeeting inputs are solicited for a problem-identification or problem-solving meeting, we usually get twenty to thirty good contributions. This will save at least thirty to sixty minutes of valuable meeting time.

Better preparation for the scheduled meeting is a second major advantage of the Delphi technique. The list of premeeting inputs stimulates our thinking. It indicates any specialized information we may want to research and bring to the meeting. It permits us to consider in advance any changes we may want to propose. And, it suggests additional ideas for us to write down to input at the meeting.

Whether the purpose of the meeting is to identify problems or to solve a problem, the premeeting list may prompt us to invite certain people to attend who would not be there otherwise. This might include specialists who can shed light on the nature and extent of specific problems or on the workability and/or requirements of certain proposals. In addition, representatives from other groups that will be or could be affected might be asked to join the meeting.

Some premeeting proposals may be so promising that we will want to reschedule the meeting to allow time to learn more about them so that we can utilize this information in our deliberations. Whatever the situation, we are likely to conduct more efficient meetings when we are guided by premeeting inputs.

Fourth Principle: Defer In-Depth Evaluation Until All Inputs Are on Display and Maintain the Display Throughout the Meeting

Deferred evaluation facilitates *brainstorming*. Brainstorming is a term for the freewheeling, uninhibited inputting of ideas. We build upon aspects of this technique to facilitate the identification of opportunities and solutions.

It pays to start with as many ideas as we can, even "halfbaked" ones. Then we can hitchhike on each other's ideas—ride on each other's coattails—to develop more and better ideas from this initial beachhead. One input stimulates another, producing a creative chain reaction. Through this process, several fragments often become a meaningful whole.

We cannot obtain good results, however, in the wrong climate. We must postpone criticism or evaluation of any idea— except for the change proposals discussed under principle eight— until all inputs are in. Research findings show that deferred judgment improves the quantity and quality of ideas (Parnes, 1967). We need to collect before we assess.

Findings show further that groups do better when they brainstorm in silence, reacting to each other's ideas as they go on display by preparing additional input cards or notes about changes they intend to propose (Van de Ven and Delbecq, 1971; Madsen and Finger, 1978).

Group Time and Effort. Premature evaluation allocates group time and effort arbitrarily. In terms of obtaining the floor, adopting a policy of first come, first served permits influential or persuasive individuals to block consideration of other inputs until their own proposals are discussed and acted upon. Unimportant matters may consume so much time that better proposals are never heard, let alone discussed.

By delaying evaluation, we put the group in control of allocating its time and effort. After seeing all of the items to be dealt with, the group may want to place a time limit on the discussion of any one item or schedule additional meetings. It may decide to appoint committees to prepare written proposals for certain items, anticipating that these will be distributed for future document review meetings. The main objective is that allocation decisions be made by the group, *not* by those who succeed in getting the floor first.

Attention Span and Recall Limitations. It is not uncommon for an enthusiastic problem-solving group to input as many as sixty items. To derive full benefit from these items, participants need the opportunity to consider and discuss each one before a decision is made. However, this cannot be done unless all inputs are recorded and displayed throughout the meeting. Research findings show that most people have an effective attention span of only seven to nine items (Miller, 1956).

Another interesting study (Fischhoff, Slovic, and Lichtenstein, 1978) documents the limitations that most of us face when it comes to recall.

One group of experienced automobile mechanics was given a "pruned" version of the complete fault tree chart shown in Figure 3; the Starting System, Ignition System, and Mischievous Acts branches were removed. They were then asked to estimate, on

Figure 3. Fault Tree of Possible Defects Causing a Car to Fail to Start.

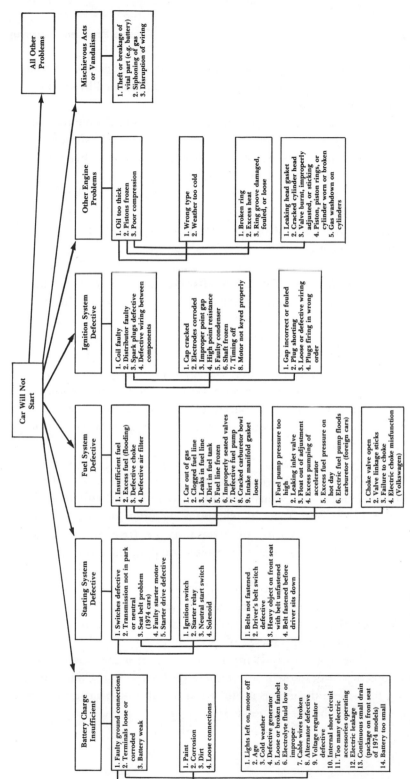

Source: From Fischhoff, B., Slovic, P., and Lichtenstein, S. "Fault Trees: Sensivity of Estimated Failure Probabilities to Problem Representation." *Journal of Experimental Psychology: Human Perception and Performance,* 1978, *4* (2). Copyright © 1978 by American Psychological Association. Used by permission.

the average: "For every 100 times that a trip is delayed due to a 'starting failure,' how many of the delays are caused by each of the four factors shown?"

They assigned 21 percent to the All Other Problems branch; whereas, mechanics given the "unpruned" version assigned a total of 44 percent to the All Other Problems branch plus the three branches that were deleted in the "pruned" fault tree. In other words, the perceived importance of the All Other Problems branch is not greatly affected by leaving out up to 50 percent of the main branches. What is out of sight tends to be out of mind, even for technical experts.

Emotionality. The silent display of sensitive items defuses the emotional potential we normally associate with confrontation. When they are first displayed, they tend to evoke nervous laughter, facetious comments, or apprehensive facial expressions. However, as they remain in view awaiting later discussion, much of this emotional potential is dissipated. The group becomes more comfortable with their presence. By the time the *discussion phase* begins, the group is prepared to deal with these issues more dispassionately than would be possible in a more conventional group setting.

Disruptive Reviews. When a group is left with unfinished business from a previous meeting, it may be difficult to pick up where it left off. Wasteful backtracking often occurs, and something of the previous meeting may be lost in the process. Typically, the longer the intervening interval, the more serious the problem.

Another problem occurs when individual participants arrive late or miss an entire meeting. Should we suspend ongoing activity for a lengthy replay, or simply forge ahead with uninformed and less productive colleagues?

The display of all inputs throughout a meeting, with any accepted changes noted, solves these problems. At a glance, anyone can tell where the group is and what of substance has gone before, however much time has passed.

The display offers another advantage; it stimulates additional inputting during a meeting. As the display grows in length, it also gives participants a sense of movement and accomplishment. Last, but perhaps not least, it prevents a person who has the floor from the gamesmanship of removing previous inputs from view (by erasing a blackboard or removing displayed charts), thereby detracting from a group's ability to relate to ideas other than those being presented.

Fifth Principle: Assure Discussion Opportunity for All Display Items Before Voting

Maintaining all inputs on display is very important, but it is not enough. We should also guarantee opportunity for all of the inputs to be discussed before any voting on their relative worth takes place for the reasons presented below. If this seems to pose an unreasonable demand for group meeting time, be reassured. In a typical meeting, some of the items on display will not stimulate discussion, and only brief comments will be directed to many others. Group members will reserve their main efforts for relatively few items. Using the procedures in this book, a typical group can process some sixty starting inputs in less than four hours.

Better Discussion. When we are assured that our ideas will have their turn before the group, we can relax and give our full attention to the discussion at hand. We will not have to worry about how we can get the floor before it is too late, as is often the case when parliamentary procedure is used. It needlessly perpetuates the first come, first served custom when it is used outside of large legislative bodies for which it was designed. Often, a seconded motion forces group members to accept or reject a position before they are ready. They are denied the opportunity to evaluate the position relative to *all* useful positions that the group might eventually develop.

Guetzkow and Gyr (1954) show that this is not merely conjectural. On the basis of their study of the use of parliamentary procedure in many groups, they found that most of the time, it did *not* facilitate movement toward genuine consensus.

Better Decisions. Agreement that all items will be discussed prevents the forcing of a judgment on any one until everyone in the group has had a chance to hear the pros and cons of all items. This need is even more important when the receipt of premeeting inputs prompts some group members to obtain additional information and leads to the inclusion of specially qualified participants at the meeting. We can realize the full potential of such resources only if we agree to avoid premature closure.

By way of contrast, think of the bandwagon effect, whereby a well organized minority can impose its will on a group. Several members, by prior agreement, make a quick succession of positive statements in support of a desired motion. Then, they call for a vote. As was pointed out in the previous chapter, one study found that the first proposal that gets fifteen more positive than negative comments is adopted 85 percent of the time, regardless of its quality, and that when a higher quality solution is presented later in the meeting, it has little chance of displacing the poorer one (Maier, 1967).

The more possible solutions that a problem-solving group can explore, not just list, the greater success it is likely to achieve. This is the conclusion drawn from a review of research studies which compare individual problem solving with group problem solving (Shaw, 1976).

Better Acceptance. When we ensure that no final choices will be made until all items have been considered, we assure everyone of an equal opportunity to influence group members. As a result, participants will feel fairly treated and will be more likely to accept and support the decisions made, whether or not their ideas are included. Support for this is provided by the studies on fair truck assignment discussed in Chapter One. In 76 percent of sixty-two groups, all group members were satisfied with the group solution when leaders let the group decide; however, in only 4 percent of twenty-four groups were all group members satisfied with the group solution when leaders were perceived as dominating the decision-making process (Maier and Hoffman, 1962).

Sixth Principal: Limit Discussion to Desired Clarification and Presentation of Pros and Cons for Display Items

Such activities as digression, needless repetition, hostile interpersonal exchanges, and hard-sell attempts to browbeat others into agreement do not help to foster a productive problem-solving environment. The quality of an idea, rather than member status or dominating behavior, should be the basis for group member voting. The discussion phase of a problem-solving meeting should be used to illuminate choices as fully as possible, *not* to engineer a superficial kind of agreement.

Some group members will simply refrain from speaking when they are faced with the likelihood of needlessly personal confrontations. Others may not have sufficient time or opportunity to contribute when such activities go unchecked. Such tendencies were revealed by a study of seventy five-member conventional discussion groups that took on the same problem of judgment. Typically, individuals and subgroups tried to "sell" their own solutions, rather than directing their energies toward building upon the best ideas that emerged (Tuckman and Lorge, 1962).

When there is group commitment up front to ban such activity as a matter of approved procedure, the leader is spared a tough dilemma: how to maintain control without appearing to get personal or to "pull rank," and thereby antagonize certain group members and chill the working climate. Most group members view the enforcement of approved rules and procedures as facilitative, not punitive.

Seventh Principle: Allow a Single Unexplained Objection to Block Any Proposed Change

If a group member is uncertain as to whether she or he will be pressured about claiming authorship of an item during a meeting, especially a sensitive item, he or she will be less inclined to input the item in the first place. At the same time, we need to satisfy principle five's requirement that in-depth evaluation of items be deferred until all items are on display. Yet, we need to facilitate the making of proposed changes to items as a meeting

progresses, so that needless repetition and ambiguous or inadequate wording can be dealt with.

Satisfaction of these needs is provided by *no-discussion
proposals for change*. At any time, any participant can propose the
rewording of an item, the combining of interdependent items, or
the elimination of an apparently duplicate item. No explanation is
required, though one may be volunteered. The matter is not
debatable or subject to a majority vote; one unexplained objection
blocks the proposed change.

This may seem like an extreme form of protection for an
individual objector, but, remember, the proposer of the change is
free to incorporate her or his ideas in a new input, and no one's
permission is required to add it to those already on display.
Consequently, no one is penalized because we prevent the
alteration or removal of another person's contribution against that
person's wishes, and no one is forced into defending his or her
turf.

Eighth Principle: Always Use Anonymous Voting

The use of a secret ballot is not new to most people, but its
importance for getting truer and more objective group sentiment
may be. Typically, a secret ballot is used only on those occasions
when a particularly sensitive issue is being voted on. At other
times, we are likely to hear: "Anyone want a secret ballot?" Reply:
"No, of course not. We're among friends; don't we trust each
other?" Or: "Why should we, we're a mature group of people,
aren't we?"

Commendable sentiment, but not very realistic. The debili-
tating factors of status and intimidation affect voting as much as
the inputting of ideas. The need may be less apparent, but it is just
as real. Omit secret balloting and collective judgments will most
assuredly be affected more by status and "going with the group"
trends.

Public voting often creates an illusion of consensus or of a
process completed, because people are reluctant to reveal their true
sentiments. This was demonstrated in a study which compared
public voting behavior with confidential responses on the same

issues. Many who participated in unanimous public votes retained quite different positions in private (Fox, 1957).

It is easy to put people on the spot by raising an issue just prior to voting. There should be advance agreement that a secret ballot will be used at *all* meetings.

Ninth Principle: Provide a Second Vote Option

There are times when the tallied results of a secret ballot are ambiguous. For example, the group's assignment of values to certain items may be much less consistent than its assignment to others. Does this represent diversity of informed judgment, or diversity that resulted from varying degrees of uninformed judgment? The latter can occur when a group lacks sufficient collective knowledge, or when informed group members do not adequately share their knowledge during the discussion phase.

Experience has shown that it is fruitful for a group to explore an ambiguous issue by setting aside the vote on such items, reopening the discussion phase for them, and then having a *second vote* on them. Under these conditions, missing information is likely to surface and the items tend to receive a more probing examination in the second effort than they received during the first discussion phase.

There is also preventive value in a second vote option. Any single method of voting is vulnerable to manipulation, as Chechile (1984) has demonstrated; however, this vulnerability can be minimized when participants know in advance that voting results will be examined and that a second vote option is always available.

We have yet to observe the need for a *third vote,* but it is conceivable. The chief concern is whether or not the group is satisfied with the process that produced the results.

In Conclusion

When we render these nine principles fully operational with the rules and procedures of Chapters Four through Nine, we will have described the best approach yet developed for problem-free problem solving. We call this approach Improved Nominal Group

Technique (INGT), a refinement of Nominal Group Technique (NGT) as developed by Delbecq, Van de Ven, and Gustafson (1975) on the basis of their extensive research.

Even in its unimproved form, NGT has been found to be superior to conventional group problem-solving procedures in over 90 percent of comparison studies (based upon literature reviews by Sullivan, 1978; Van de Ven, 1982; and, more recently, the author). Our tests of the improved form, INGT, in many different ongoing groups have produced even more conclusive results: In *all* instances to date, most participants have indicated, anonymously, that they prefer INGT to their current methods.

The next six chapters will present easy-to-implement answers to such questions as:

- What practical means can we use to assure anonymity of authorship when we collect inputs?
- What instructions should we give concerning premeeting activity?
- What physical arrangements should we make before a meeting?
- How should inputs be displayed?
- How, specifically, should we conduct a meeting so that the principles will be fully satisfied?
- What are the "nuts and bolts" of sound voting?
- How are procedures modified for a document review meeting?
- How should we coordinate two or more groups working on the same assignment concurrently?

Chapter Four

Premeeting Idea Generation and Preparation

We should plan to deal with only *one* of the following purposes in any given meeting: identifying and prioritizing problems, positions, or options; solving a particular problem; or debugging or refining a written proposal or other document.

Whenever possible, the meeting should be called far enough in advance to permit participants to deliberate about their premeeting inputs before writing them, *anonymously,* on 3 x 5 cards to be deposited in a conveniently located, slotted box by a deadline that will accommodate the other premeeting activities described below. Participants should be instructed to cover different ideas in separate input statements, although several statements may be written on one card.

Sufficient time should be allowed after the deadline to type up a numbered list of all input statements submitted without combining, editing, or revising them in any way. The list should then be duplicated and distributed to the participants in time to allow compliance with premeeting instructions along the following lines: "Please prepare a reminder list to bring to the meeting of any proposals you plan to make for changing the wording of any item, or for combining any items on the distributed list. Also, please jot down any additional items which occur to you on 3 x 5 cards (as many items to a card as you like) to input anonymously at the beginning of the meeting. In addition, be sure to bring this distributed list to the meeting, since it will serve as our display of premeeting inputs." There is no need to place the items obtained in any particular order before numbering them and typing up the list, since the only purpose of numbering is to give each item a unique identity for the purposes of discussion, the handling of proposed changes, and voting. Take extra copies of the distributed list of inputs to the meeting, for it is likely that at least one person will forget to bring it.

Even when there is not enough time to solicit, duplicate, and distribute inputs before a meeting, it is still useful to announce the purpose of the meeting in advance and to ask participants to complete 3 x 5 input cards before they arrive. This will save valuable group time by permitting an anonymous collection of cards at the very beginning of the meeting.

Tailor the Announcement to the Purpose

We should have a single purpose for the meeting, and the announcement to participants should leave no doubt as to what that purpose is. Some examples of how announcements for the different purposes might be worded are presented below.

Identifying Problems, Positions, or Options. If the purpose of the meeting is to identify problems, the announcement can be put in the form of a question: "What problems do you feel interfere with the effective functioning of our group (organization)?" Or, it can be put in the form of a request: "Please list all the problems that you feel currently interfere with our functioning."

Use of an open-ended request avoids the danger of limiting contributions on the basis of our own concerns or perceptions. For example, if we ask "What are the motivational problems?" or "What are the problems with working conditions?" we risk not learning about other important possibilities.

If the purpose of the meeting is to identify options or positions, the request might be worded: "Please list the options (positions) which you feel are relevant to our present situation." If there are special conditions in your present situation that must be satisfied and may not be known to some participants, they should be stated in the announcement.

> *Example from Practice.* The assistant deputy for contracting and manufacturing at an air force base was concerned about the morale and efficiency of his largely civilian directorate, but he didn't know quite where to start in dealing with the situation. As a consultant, the author agreed to hold a meeting with his subordinates, using the procedures presented in this book, on the topic: "What problems or conditions keep us from operating more efficiently and effectively?" They identified six key problem areas from a much larger list, and they successfully solved each one through a series of meetings, addressing one problem per meeting.
>
> Despite the absence of an opportunity to gain the benefits of premeeting inputting and the fact that this was their first exposure to the procedures discussed in this book, eleven of the twelve participants strongly endorsed this new approach—through anonymous balloting—in preference to their customary approach.

Solving a Problem. The announcement for a meeting to solve a particular problem might say: "One of the top priority problems (problem areas) identified in our meeting of (such and such a date) is (statement of problem). Please contribute, anonymously, as many solutions or solution approaches as you can suggest. The special conditions that a potential solution must satisfy are (list conditions). The special characteristics that will improve the value of any given solutions are (list characteristics)."

The statement of special conditions or characteristics is included only if it presents information that group members are not likely to have or if it serves as a needed reminder.

Before sending out an announcement for a meeting, it is a good practice to verify that the statement of the problem really communicates what you intended. Show it to several people who have not seen it before, and have them tell you what it includes and/or requests.

Example from Practice. The employees of a university hospital were hurt by inflation because legislative funding had been low for several years. Now that there was additional money, there was a big debate. Should all of it be used for catch-up or cost-of-living adjustments, or should there also be merit increases? Supervisors differed strongly on this issue.

With the author guiding group leaders in the use of this book's procedures, thirty-six supervisors met in several groups at a weekend retreat to deal with this potentially explosive issue. Many good ideas had already been inputted, duplicated, and distributed during the premeeting phase. In just one evening, group discussions were completed, and the results were melded into an acceptable total group solution. (This goal was accomplished through use of the multiple group procedures to be discussed in Chapter Nine.)

The most striking outcome occurred in a meeting of the supervisors which took place after they had implemented the agreed-on plan and had discussed the resulting pay adjustments with each subordinate. The hospital administrator asked if anyone was dissatisfied in any way with the plan. No sign of displeasure was given. This contrasted dramatically with the open dissension that had occurred at a preretreat meeting of the same group.

Reviewing a Document. The written proposal, or other document, should be duplicated and distributed in advance with the following type of announcement: "Please study the enclosed and contribute any ideas you have, anonymously, on how it can be improved upon. Please identify, also possible problems, whether or not you have any possible solution in mind."

If the document review meeting produces suggested changes that require further study or that require coordination with people outside of the group before they can be adopted, the final versions of these changes should be submitted to a special document review meeting.

> *Example from Practice.* A local minister was being pressured by one group of deacons and elders to change certain church rules, policies, and procedures. At the same time, another faction wanted just as ardently to keep them unchanged.
>
> At the suggestion of the author, a document review meeting was scheduled for a group of twenty representatives of the two factions. The existing *Rules, Policies, and Procedures Manual* was distributed two weeks before the meeting, with the question: "How can we improve upon this?" Inputs were typed, duplicated, and distributed in advance, with the request that participants consider changes to the inputs that they would like to propose at the meeting, as well as any additional inputs they might wish to make.
>
> At the meeting, proposed changes that met with no objections were adopted without further deliberation. Those that met with one or more objections were voted upon at the end of the meeting, after group members had been given ample opportunity to present pros and cons for each. A secret, majority vote was used to decide the fate of each proposed change. Problems that needed further investigation and/or deliberation were assigned to subsequent problem-solving meetings for solution. In this way, the *Rules, Policies, and Procedures Manual* was updated and strengthened with surprisingly little dissension.

Obtain Needed Equipment and Supplies

Have three flipchart stands with pads on hand to prevent the transcription of 3 x 5 card inputs during the meeting from becoming a bottleneck. Do *not* plan to use a blackboard for several reasons: (1) there is often insufficient room; (2) several people can more readily transcribe on separate flipcharts than on one blackboard; and (3) flipchart pages provide a permanent, easily transportable record of what took place.

Reserve a room for the meeting in a quiet location. It should have adequate wall space to display six to seven flipchart pages where participants can readily see them. Chairs should be arranged in a "U" pattern around a table on which participants can write, with room for the leader and three flipchart stands at the open end of the "U."

You will need to obtain magic markers or other means for writing on the flipcharts. Whatever you plan to use, give it a pre-meeting check to see if seated participants will be able to read what is written with it. In addition, pencils and at least five 3 x 5 cards for each participant will be required. And, masking tape with which to hang filled flipchart pages on the wall should be on hand.

Chapter Five

In-Meeting Idea Generation and Refinement

When it is likely that participants have brought inputs on 3 x 5 cards to submit at the meeting, the first order of business is for the leader to collect the cards in a way that will assure anonymity of authorship. He or she announces a *card collection round,* requesting that *everyone* contribute a card (blank or otherwise) face down to a pile in the center of the table and urges the preparation of new cards as additional inputs are stimulated by those items being transcribed on flipchart pages and displayed. The collection round is repeated every five to ten minutes, until all cards submitted are blank.

Comments by the leader for this initial inputting phase might proceed as follows.

Leader: The guidelines we are trying out call for inputting your ideas, anonymously, and getting them all on display before we discuss the pros and cons of any of them. (Leader distributes blank cards to everyone.)

Since some of you have brought completed cards with you, let's start off with a card collection round. Will everyone please put a card face down in the center of the table for me to pick up. If you don't have a card with an idea on it right now, just submit a blank one. This precaution of getting a facedown card from everyone will become more important, in terms of protecting your anonymity, in later collection rounds when only a few people are still submitting ideas.

While the cards collected are now being transcribed to flipchart pages for display, you will have a *silent writing period* of five to ten minutes to prepare cards for another collection round. You can put as many ideas as you wish on one card, but, remember, do not identify yourself.

In writing down (problems, options, positions, solutions, proposed changes to a document, or questions—depending upon the purpose of the meeting) be as specific as you can. For example, if you write (for a problem-identification meeting) that "senior people get too much of the overtime work," we will have a better fix on your thinking than if you write: "the way that overtime is handled." Put different ideas in separate input statements on the card. As you will see when we vote, having too few choices poses more of a problem than having too many.

Don't worry about being completely original. If any ideas on the premeeting distribution list or on the flipchart pages suggest additional ideas, or what you feel are improved versions, let's have them. (Leader passes out premeeting list of contributed ideas to anyone who does not have it.)

As the leader performs (or oversees) the transcription and display of items from the cards to flipchart pages, he or she observes the writing activity of participants to determine when another card collection round will be appropriate.

When no premeeting announcement of purpose and inputting of ideas is used, the leader starts the meeting with an announcement of purpose; distributes blank cards; gives the instructions presented above; and delays the first card collection round until after participants have had a sufficient silent writing period to put some ideas on the cards.

A meeting to clarify written materials or verbal directives is usually simple and straightforward. There is no need to use the procedures presented in this book. A verbal summary is given and questions are invited and answered.

However, even for this type of meeting, we should not overlook the potential value of anonymous inputting. People may wish to present sensitive questions as well as sensitive problems. At the beginning of a meeting when participants may have such questions, they should at least be asked to submit their questions on 3 x 5 cards, anonymously. In this way, they are encouraged to share their real concerns.

Transcription and Display

After everyone places a facedown card in the central pile, the leader mixes them before picking them up to assure anonymity of authorship for the last ones turned in and for those placed in a particular position. Then the leader sorts out the blank ones for reuse and determines how many items there are for transcription to flipchart pages. At this stage, it is important to keep in mind the need to have a separate display item for each distinctly different idea, even if the contributor combined ideas on the input card.

If there are more than five or six items to transcribe, the leader shares the cards with other group members or with secretaries standing by to help, to facilitate transcription of the items to the several available flipcharts without creating a bottleneck.

As a rule, we should *not* edit or reword contributions as we transcribe them. If we do, contributors may feel that we are trying to show them up, or they may feel embarrassed and will be less inclined to make further contributions.

An exception to this rule is the needlessly wordy contribution. For example, a statement such as: "One of the big problems which confronts us in this organization, and confronts many other organizations for that matter, is one of inadequate communications" should be transcribed to the flipchart simply as "inadequate communications."

However, do not omit anything if there is doubt about the effect it will have upon meaning: If in doubt, do not leave it out. With most participants, a lack of clarity is a temporary problem. They begin to make their inputs more concise when they see the value of doing so.

When more than one person is transcribing inputs from the cards to flipchart pages, we want to be sure that each item is given a different number to make identification easy. A simple way to do this is for one person to number the items he or she transcribes as 1A, 2A, 3A, and so on; while another uses 1B, 2B, 3B; and another 1C, 2C, 3C. Assuming that items on a premeeting distribution list are numbered without letters, each item will have its own number or number/letter combination. There is no need for the numbers to be consecutive.

As each flipchart page is filled with inputs, it should be attached to the wall with masking tape where everyone can see it. All inputs should be on display throughout the meeting.

No-Discussion Proposals for Change

We have agreed to put off any evaluative discussion of inputs until all of them are on display to encourage everyone to contribute. This rule, however, should not constrain the group to work with needless repetition or ambiguous wording which no one wants.

At any time, any participant should be permitted to propose the rewording of an item, the combination of interdependent items, or the elimination of apparently duplicate items. No discussion or explanation is required. For example, someone may propose that item 6B be dropped because it duplicates item 2A; or that a certain phrase be substituted for a word in item 15 on the premeeting list; or that items 4 and 16C be combined into one item.

The leader says: "It is proposed that such and such be done, is there any objection?" If *one* hand goes up, the change is blocked. No explanation is required from the objector, although he or she is free to volunteer one. The matter is not debatable, nor is it subject to a majority vote. One unexplained objection stops the proposal in its tracks. However, the proposer is free to incorporate the proposed change in a new input, and no one's permission is required to get it on display before the group.

Two cautions are in order which may not be apparent to first-time users of these guidelines. One, items should be grouped together because the resulting combined item is superior, *not* because items *can* be grouped that way. Distinctly separate ideas should be presented as separate items to permit participants to rank their preferences adequately when they vote. We should aim in the direction of too many items to choose from rather than too few. Two, no-discussion proposals should be made with restraint. Our main purpose during the first part of the meeting is to encourage contributions, not to enter into a game of "Who Can Make the Most Changes?"

The leader should let the group know that no-discussion proposals may be made, but should not call for them or in any other way promote them. He or she should make it clear to the group that the purpose of a no-discussion proposal is not merely the consolidation of items for the sake of consolidation, nor the elimination of an item simply because someone doesn't like it.

A group member may say: "I feel that the wording of item 16C can be improved upon," expecting that this will start a discussion that will lead to suggestions from others. However, no discussion proposals for change are made by individuals, not by discussion and majority vote.

The leader should respond: "Our procedure requires *you* to make the proposed change and not the group as a whole or some other participant. If you need more time to develop the wording, just let me know when you are ready to put it before the group."

If the person plans to propose a lengthy change, the leader should ask that it be written on a separate flipchart page, or submitted on a card for transcription to the flipchart page, so that no one will be in doubt as to the exact nature of the proposal.

Whether proposals are verbal or written, it is useful for the leader to repeat them out loud to the group before asking if there is any objection to making the change. If there is no objection, the change should be noted immediately beside the item or items affected, either on the premeeting distribution list (with all participants entering the change) or on the flipchart page or pages (with the leader entering the change).

Deletions should be noted in a way that will permit us to read what was deleted. A light "X" over an entire item or a light line through part of an item does the job nicely.

Discussion Phase

When the last card collection round turns up all blank cards, we are ready to move to phase 2 of the meeting: discussion of the items on display. This move, however, should not close the door on the making of no-discussion proposals for change or on the inputting of new items. The leader states that any additional items can be given verbally or in writing by anyone at any time, unless someone requests another card collection round. If another round is requested, the leader should comply. However, such a request is unusual since it is likely that the need for anonymity will have been satisfied by this stage of the meeting.

Chapter Six

Guiding the
Discussion Phase Effectively

When the last card collection round turns up all blank cards, and all items are on display, it may appear that we will not have enough time for adequately discussing them and for final voting during the remainder of the present meeting. Should we place a time limit on the discussion of each item? Or, can we avoid the handicap of a time limit by extending the time of the present meeting, or by calling an additional meeting?

The leader should present these choices and have the decision determined by majority vote. It is *not* the role of the leader to make decisions for the group in a participative meeting. Rather, it is the leader's job to create and maintain a climate that facilitates wholehearted participation.

The matter might be presented in the following manner:

Leader: We're ready now to move into the discussion phase of our meeting, since all of the facedown cards in the last collection round were blank.

As you can see, we have fifty-five items on display. We've agreed to provide discussion opportunity for all of these, but we've also agreed to end the meeting today at 5:00 p.m.—just ninety minutes from now. So, we have a decision to make about how we will proceed.

It is likely that no one will want to discuss some of the items; still, a time limit for discussing each could really handicap us, and we don't need a limit to keep people from wasting time. The guidelines we are following will do that.

But the decision is up to you. Do we set a limit? Can we stay longer today? Or, can we schedule another meeting this week? The display sheets do make it easy to pick up again from where we stop. What's your pleasure?

Discussion should follow, with the group voting on what to do. The main idea is that the group, rather than any individual, is in charge of the allocation of its time and efforts.

Discussion Guidelines

We will be able to keep discussion on track without wasting time, while encouraging the kind of genuine participation we want, by committing ourselves to the following guidelines:

- The purpose of the discussion phase is to provide an opportunity for anyone to seek or give clarification as to what an item means, and to give reasons for being for or against an item. All other activity, other than offering no-discussion proposals for change, is ruled out of order by the leader.
- Participants may seek explanation from a presenter as to how her or his ideas would deal with a particular need or difficulty, and they make ask for repetition of an idea; however, it is *not* our purpose to formally debate the merits of an item, reach agreement about an item, or to persuade others to adopt our viewpoint through speech making or repetition.
- A contributor may voluntarily claim authorship of an item, but any kind of inquiry about authorship is out of order.
- A participant may add a new item to the display list at any time before the final voting. Verbal inputting may be used, unless the contributor requests a card collection round; however, any items contributed by the leader should be made anonymously.

- The leader will continue to accept no-discussion proposals for change throughout the meeting.
- The leader will go through the entire list of items, inviting comment item by item, *before any voting* on them takes place. This may require a time limit on discussion of each item or the scheduling of additional meeting time.
- There will be no obligation to discuss any item, only the assured opportunity.
- At any time, a person may return to a previous item for further discussion, as long as the total discussion time on that item does not exceed any set limit.

Applying the Guidelines

Since these guidelines will be new to most people, they should be communicated effectively and enforced by the leader when necessary. At the very least, a list of guidelines should be distributed at the beginning of the meeting.

Whatever the case, get your group to give these guidelines a fair trial by making no attempt to change them in midstream. They may seem strange at first, but this initial reaction will not last. The group, in all probability, will become comfortable with them and appreciate the results obtained.

Commentary during the discussion phase of the meeting might take place as follows.

Leader: Okay, we're ready to move into the discussion phase of our meeting, since all of the facedown cards from the last collection round were blank. Remember, discussion is for seeking or providing clarification about what an item means and for speaking for or against an item. It is *not* for arguing with each other or for trying to reach total agreement about each item.

You can still propose eliminating or changing an item at any time, but it will take only one raised hand to block the change, with no explanation needed. You are also free to add a new item to the display list at any time, with no one's permission required. If you don't want to input an item verbally, let me know and we'll have another card collection round.

If there are no questions about procedure, let's start. (Leader refers to item 1 on the premeeting distribution list, if there was one; otherwise, he or she addresses the first item on display on the wall by reading it aloud to the group.) Any comment on item 1?

Group member 3: Yes, it says the problem is inadequate communications. Just what does that mean? Communication with whom and by whom?

Leader: We have a request for clarification of item 1. Anyone care to respond? The fact that you do won't necessarily mean it's your item. In fact, we don't want to know whose item it is, unless the author wants us to know.

Group member 6: Well, it's not mine, but what it means to me is that we are not kept adequately informed about developments outside of our group which affect our work.

Group member 4: That's what it means to me, too, and I propose that we change item 1 to read that way.

Leader: We have a proposal to change item 1, "Inadequate communications," to read: "Not kept adequately informed about developments outside our group which affect our work." Is there any objection to this change? (Waiting, and observing no hand go up to object, the leader draws a light line through "Inadequate communications," or asks participants to do so if it is on a handout list. He or she then writes in the new wording below the item, or at the end of the list if there is not enough space, still numbering it as item 1.)

Any discussion of item 1 as it now stands? (One person describes how it affects his particular job. Another describes the frustration of being in the dark.) Any comment on item 2, "Assignment of overtime work is unfair to newcomers"?

Group member 2 (a long-service employee): Who's griping about that? Must be a newcomer who isn't willing to pay his dues like the rest of us have. (No one in the group responds.) Well, whatsamatta, are you afraid to speak up?

Leader: Now come on, Charley, being afraid has nothing to do with it. We agreed to follow the guidelines, and the guidelines say that we will not try to find out who the author of an item is. Let's give the guidelines a fair chance as we agreed, okay? After we see how they work out, we can decide whether or not we want to keep them. Now, any discussion on item 2? (Leader pauses and there is no response.) Any comments on item 3, "Work areas are not kept clean enough"? (Several group members comment on item 3.)

Group Member 8:   I just thought of another problem I want to get up there. Can I just give it to you verbally without having to write it on a card?

Leader: Sure, Joe. After the initial collection of anonymous inputs, it's up to the individual. I'm going to have one last card collection round when we finish with the last item on display. Anyone who wants to can wait for that, and any new items that come in will be discussed in the same way as those inputted at the beginning. Any further comments on item 3? (No response.) Alright, what about item 4, "The present tool checkout system causes unnecessary bottlenecks"?

Group member 3:   Just a minute. I made some pretty important comments about how serious item 3 is and the group didn't seem much concerned. Maybe I didn't make my case clear enough? (Starts to repeat the same points he had made before.)

Leader: Hold on, Bill. Do you have anything to add to what you said before?

Group member 3:   No, but I don't think they understand.

Leader: Well, let's check with the group. Our guidelines say no repetition unless a group member wants it. Anyone feel a need for Bill to repeat his position? (No response.) Sorry, Bill, but unless you have something to add, I'll have to rule that out of order.

And so it goes. The leader functions primarily as a facilitator of productive group action by enforcing these proven guidelines that the group has agreed to give a fair trial.

The leader will not be viewed as a facilitator, however, if participants feel that he or she tries to impose personal preferences or arbitrary judgments on the group. Consequently, the leader's safest course is to present ideas anonymously, limiting his or her contributions during the discussion phase to the presentation of important considerations, such as established constraints that must be met, rather than taking strong stands.

In Chapter Seven, we will look at the last phase of activity: voting on the final form of the item display list.

Chapter Seven

Voting Procedures
for Authentic Results

Before voting takes place, *all* contributions should be collected, displayed, and discussed. In addition, it may pay to give more than passing thought to exactly what group members will be asked to vote for. If the purpose of the meeting is to identify problems, the question for the *first vote* might be "What are the five most important problem items to you?" (A way to determine the appropriate number of items to ask for is presented later in this chapter.)

On some occasions, especially when a large number of items is under consideration, participants may prefer to classify the items into categories before voting. Such categories might include: problems which can be solved by our group; problems which must be solved through collaboration with people outside of our group; and problems which must be solved by others, who may or may not solicit our advice.

Participants then vote on the three to five most important items in each category. As we will see, having each person vote for just a few items will reveal more than just what the several top-level choices are.

If the purpose of the meeting is to solve a given problem, the voting question is "Which of these solutions are acceptable to you?" We would then ask participants to list up to three items by number in the order of perceived importance, placing the most important at the top of the list. In a *second vote,* the finalist solutions may be ranked again; or, as an alternative, the solution that receives the most *yes* votes is the winner, assuming that the number of positives is equal to at least 51 percent of the voters. (Voting procedure for a document review meeting is discussed in Chapter Eight.)

First Vote

One vote is usually enough. Sometimes, however, it is useful to have additional discussion and a second vote for reasons we will discuss. Research has shown that discovering the true sense of a group's position is aided by having each participant submit a score, so that group judgment can be expressed as a total of such scores. A simple way to do this, satisfactory for most occasions, is to have each participant pick a given number of most important items and rank-order them.

A rule of thumb for determining the appropriate number of most important items to request is to take 15 percent of all items remaining before the group when it is time to vote. Table 2 may be used in place of the computation.

Alternation Ranking Technique. The use of *alternation ranking* yields better results than having participants list items in descending order from most important to least important. Having picked the items to be ranked, the procedure is (1) choose the *most important* item; (2) choose the *least important* item; (3) choose the *second most important* item; (4) choose the *second least important item;* and so on.

Studies show that alternation ranking is associated with high reliability, as measured by interjudge agreement and by intrajudge consistency (Henry, 1962; McMurry, 1963).

Handling Ties. To permit ties, we need to assure that each voter will use the same number of total points. Otherwise, some voters can exert a disproportionate influence. Steps can be taken to prevent such situations. When voters feel that two items are of equal importance, they should be instructed to take an average of

Table 2. Determining the Number of Items to Rank.

Number of Finalist Items	Number of Most Important Items to Request
23	3
24–30	4
31–36	5
37–43	6
44–50	7
51–56	8
57–63	9
64 or more	10

their rank values and assign that average value to each of the two items that are tied. Take, for instance, the sample ballot card shown in Figure 4. If the voter thinks that item #3 and item #4 are tied, he or she should put 2.5 (2 + 3/2) by each item. If the voter thinks that #8 and #16 are tied for most important item, he or she should put 4.5 (5 + 4/2) by each.

In a three-way tie, one-third of the sum of the three items is assigned to each. For example, assuming that items #8, #16, and #4 are tied, each gets 4 points. With this approach, all voters have the same total points (15 in this example) to distribute among the items to be ranked (in this case five).

Conducting the Voting. Assume we have thirty-four finalist problems when we are ready to vote. Following the 15 percent rule, five items are to be chosen for ranking. The leader's comments might go as follows:

Leader (passing out blank 3 x 5 cards for use as ballots): We've finished our discussion of all the items, so it's time to vote. Please select the five problems you feel are most important, without consulting anyone. We want your private, independent vote. If you have difficulty reading any of the sheets on the wall, feel free to get up and move closer. Be sure to consider *all* items before making your selection.

You need put only the *numbers* of the five items you select. You don't have to write them out on a 3 x 5 card. Next, put a

Figure 4. Sample Ballot A.

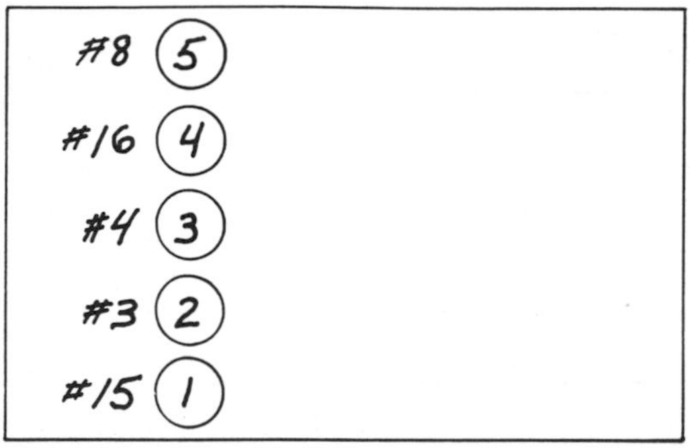

circled "5" by the most important item on your card, a circled "4" by the next most important item, and so on. The circling will help to avoid confusing rank value and item number when the results are tallied.

(To make the instructions clearer, the leader can draw a sample ballot [see Figure 4] for the group on a flipchart. Note that the circled value given to the most important item is always equal to the number of items the participants are asked to select.)

Studies show that a most effective way to rank the items is to use a procedure called alternation ranking. To do this, first, choose the most important item; second, the least important; third, the second most important; fourth, the second least important, and so on.

(If ties are permitted, add:) If you feel that two items are tied, assign each an average value; in other words, give half of the sum of their rank values to each. In a three-way tie, give one-third of the sum to each. (Pointing to the sample ballot on display:) For example, if I felt that #8 was tied for most important item with #16, I'd put 4.5 by each: Half of the sum of their rank values, which is 9. When you finish your ballot, please turn it over and put it in the center of the table to keep the voting secret.

When all of the ballots are in, the leader mixes them around to avoid any suspicion that the last participants to put their cards on the pile might be identified. Then, with the help of a group

Figure 5. Voting Tally on Flipchart Page.

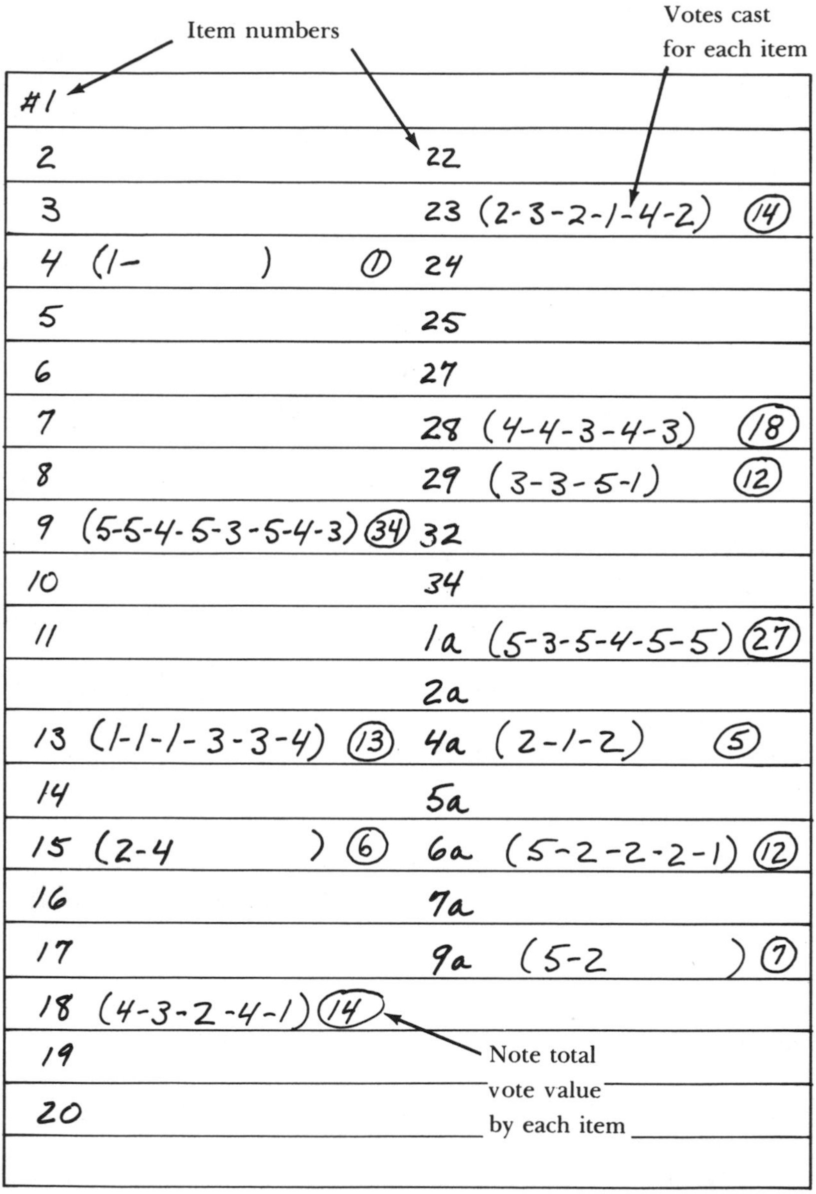

Item numbers

Votes cast
for each item

#1		
2	22	
3	23 (2-3-2-1-4-2)	⑭
4 (1-) ①	24	
5	25	
6	27	
7	28 (4-4-3-4-3)	⑱
8	29 (3-3-5-1)	⑫
9 (5-5-4-5-3-5-4-3) ㉞	32	
10	34	
11	1a (5-3-5-4-5-5) ㉗	
	2a	
13 (1-1-1-3-3-4) ⑬	4a (2-1-2)	⑤
14	5a	
15 (2-4) ⑥	6a (5-2-2-2-1)	⑫
16	7a	
17	9a (5-2)	⑦
18 (4-3-2-4-1) ⑭		
19	Note total	
20	vote value	
	by each item	

member, the leader tallies the values assigned to each item. One person can dictate the values, as the other writes them down by item number on a flipchart page, such as the one shown in Figure 5.

Usually, the first vote will produce five or six winning items that clearly have higher scores than the other items. The results are conclusive; there is no need for further action. There are times, however, when the results of the first vote raise doubts as to their true meaning. Figure 5 illustrates such a case. Looking at the total vote values, there are only three clear winners: item #9, with 34 points; item #1a, with 27 points; and item #28, with 18 points.

Five items (#13, #18, #23, #29, and #6a) are bunched together, with vote values ranging from 12 to 14 points, and the assignment of rank values to them is less consistent than to the three winning items. This inconsistency may represent differences in judgment, or it may represent differences in the interpreted meaning of various items. The latter could result from some voters having information that was not shared with the group during the discussion phase of the meeting.

Second Vote

When the first vote produces such clustered near winners, rather than five or six clear-cut winners based upon more consistent rank assignments by voters, it is useful to reopen discussion of the clustered items in preparation for a second vote about them.

A leader presenting the results of the illustrated ballot might say:

Leader: When we look at the results of the voting we see three clear-cut winners (#9, #1a, and #28), but then we have five items that compete for fourth place: #13, #18, #23, #29, and #6a. In addition, the voting is inconsistent, ranging from first or second place votes to last-place votes for the same item.

If the group is willing, we would probably benefit from reopening the discussion on these five items. Perhaps we can find out why we had so much variation in the ranks assigned to them. When we are finished with the renewed discussion opportunity for these five items and any new ones submitted, we can have a second vote to see if the consensus of the group falls more clearly into place.

Assuming that the group agrees to the additional effort, the leader reopens discussion on the five clustered items, accepting new items and proposals for changing items, as before.

The second vote is conducted in the same way as the first. However, if there are only five or six finalist items, participants can just as easily rank all of them this time to determine their relative importance before listing them below the three clear-cut winning items from the first vote. We have yet to witness a desire for a third vote, but the need is conceivable.

If the items were not classified into different categories *before* the voting (see page 60), the group may find it useful to classify winning items at this point to facilitate planning for future action.

When dealing with solutions, two or three clear-cut winners will usually emerge from the first vote. If participants prefer, an alternative to ranking these to determine *the* best solution is to have them put *yes* or *no* by each on a 3 x 5 card ballot. The solution that receives the most *yes* votes is then the winner (assuming that the total is equal to at least 51 percent of the number of voters).

No Optimal Formal Procedure

Concern about voting procedures dates back to at least the eighteenth century and the work of Borda (1781) and Condorcet (1785). More recently, Arrow's theorem (Arrow, 1951) demonstrated that no formal method can meet all criteria of rationality and fairness, absolutely. Chechile (1984) also points out the limitations of "one method, one vote."

However, the approach presented here (rank scores with tally inspection and second vote option) provides the advantages of the Borda method, while minimizing its weaknesses, namely, susceptibility to manipulation when voters can form coalitions to impose subgroup preferences upon the majority.

When we agree that no voting will occur until all inputs are on display and have been offered for discussion, it is difficult for any participant to know in advance what all of the final voting options will be. If inconsistencies are found in the assignment of rank values to particular items, it becomes a matter for discussion, clarification, and a possible second vote. Under these conditions, manipulation is unlikely if not impossible.

Adjusting for Intergroup Comparisons

We may want to compare how different groups vote when they are working on the same topic or purpose. For example, several groups in the same division of an organization may be asked: "What are the most important trends we will be faced with in five years?" It could be useful to compare the finalist items the groups come up with and how they rank them.

If the number of voters or the number of finalist items ranked varies from group to group, we need to make some adjustments to ensure a fair comparison. If only group size varies (each group ranking the same number of items), average rank scores will do the job (total score for each item divided by the number of voters). But, if the number of items ranked varies, we need to make an additional adjustment. The supplement at the end of the chapter presents a method for doing this.

Greater Accuracy with Rating Scales

The alternation ranking procedure is sufficiently accurate for most situations. However, using rating scales can increase accuracy if participants have both a basis and a need for making finer distinctions.

The key limitation with the use of rank ordering involves the unequal intervals between ranks. Suppose we have a ballot such as the one in Figure 6. Having no more information than the voter, we must treat the *preference gaps* between the items as equal. Yet we know this is rarely true. The voter may have preferred item #8 only slightly over #16, but have preferred #3

Figure 6. Sample Ballot B.

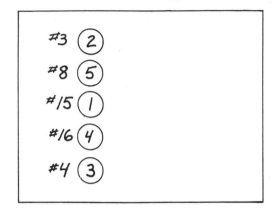

strongly over #15. And, he or she may have regarded #4 as almost tied with #3.

These problems can be avoided by rating each item on a scale from "1" to "9," with "1" being the least important and "9" the most important. The leader can display such a scale on a flipchart so that each voter can use it to pick a scale value for every item on his or her ballot. Then, either a total or an average score can be computed for each item on the tally.

A nine-degree scale is recommended because research shows that it provides a good balance between accuracy and the number of distinctions which most of us can reasonably make (Miller, 1956; Huber and Delbecq, 1972).

Although the use of rating scales takes care of the problem of preference gaps, it opens the door to possible manipulation by one or more individuals. A voter may try to impose his or her preferences by giving a value of "9" to all choices. In turn, other voters may do the same in an effort to protect themselves, and honest voting is displaced by gamesmanship.

Of course, inspection of the ballots could expose such action and the group could then decide how to deal with the problem. One possible solution, the assignment of points, is discussed below.

Point Assignment

Each voter gets the same number of points, say 100, to allot to the items being evaluated. This keeps individuals from having differing levels of power in voting. However, it does not prevent the gamesmanship of giving most of one's points to one item, not because it is that much more important but simply to get it adopted. For example, given five items to evaluate, one could give 96 points to one and only 1 point to each of the other four.

When it is not abused, this approach has the same advantage as rating scales in showing the extent to which preference gaps between ranks are not equal. Ranking will not reveal such inequalities; on the other hand, ranking prevents gamesmanship in voting and assures equal influence for each voter.

Social Participatory Allocative Network

Is there some way to achieve a single, manageable voting procedure given that members agree that certain group members are better qualified to judge the finalist items than others, and that those who are better qualified to judge will not have equal confidence in each of their judgments? Yes, there is and the procedure is called Social Participatory Allocative Network, or SPAN III.

The initial step in SPAN III is to give a quota of points to each voter. He or she then allocates the points to the items and/or to other group members. In addition, each voter can indicate her or his confidence in the allocations made to the items.

In the next step, normally handled by a computer, the points given to other group members are assigned to their item choices in the same proportions and with the same degrees of confidence with which those group members cast their own original votes for the items. Total point value for each item then equals the sum of the first *and* second step point assignments.

Unquestionably, this elaborate procedure offers unique advantages, given circumstances which warrant its use. However, the feature which permits the allocation of points to other participants can turn to disadvantage when the allocation is based upon factors other than a true difference in ability to judge the choices at hand.

A simpler alternative is discussed in Chapter Eight. The group can ask its most knowledgeable member or subgroup members to prepare a written proposal for the group to consider in a document review meeting.

SPAN III is written in FORTRAN IV for the Control Data Corporation CDC-6400 computer. It has a field length requirement of 110,000 (octal) 60-bit words, but this varies with the number of group members and the number of SPAN III features used. The program is presented in a form that facilitates adaptation to other computers (MacKinnon and Anderson, 1976).

Preserving All Display Materials

When the final voting tallies are entered beside the items on the flipchart pages, we have a complete record of the significant results of group activity. These materials should be retained. With little effort they can be redisplayed to provide an unequaled means for briefing nonparticipants about the total array of items considered, deletions and changes that were made, and the allocation of votes. This information is now a matter of record, not subject to conjecture and selective recall.

The completed pages are also valuable to chairpersons or busy executives who must keep in touch with and build on the work of several groups. Such information greatly facilitates their assessments of what has taken place and what remains to be done.

Written minutes are more difficult to prepare and only rarely are they as useful. We read about outcomes and wonder how they were arrived at. Were good alternatives considered? Was adequate attention given to their discussion and refinement? Were final decisions made in an acceptable way? Completed flipchart pages provide a better basis for answering such questions.

Before leaving, the leader should see that all display materials are placed together and rolled up for storage (after folding over or cutting off the adhesive tape, of course).

Example from Practice. A high ranking official was skeptical about whether or not his organization should continue with a program of flexible working hours (flextime) after a year's trial. Employees clearly liked it, and their union was mounting pressure for continuation. There were claims of improved performance, but no clear-cut evidence to support them. True, tardiness and absenteeism had declined; on the other hand, no one denied that unit supervisors were burdened with far more difficult scheduling problems.

The official's chief concern was whether or not the benefits of the program justified this added burden on the supervisors. He knew from experience that one-time verbal inquiries can produce very misleading results. Most managers will play it safe with a high-level officer from headquarters, until they can figure out which way the wind is blowing. The annual, anonymous organizational survey was not due for another three months and, even then, would have to be modified to obtain response data about the program from supervisors.

As a consultant to one division of the organization, I was told of the official's concern and of his impending visit to the division in two weeks. Divisional management and I had planned to have problem-solving meetings with several groups of employees and several groups of supervisors, using the procedures presented in this book and devoted to the topic: How can we improve upon the functioning of flextime? In addition, we had planned to ask the supervisory groups at the end of their sessions to indicate, anonymously, whether or not they favored continuing the program. Consequently, we held the meetings right away and used the flipchart pages and voting tallies to brief the official upon his arrival.

When he entered the briefing room, he was visibly impressed by the ease with which he could

reconstruct the participants' concerns and actions
without having been present. Most of all, he valued
being able to treat the materials as an accurate
representation of the real views of the participants,
because they had inputted them anonymously.

Supplement

On occasion, we may wish to compare the final voting
results for different groups which will not meet again in order to
discuss and to vote upon a consolidated listed of finalist items
compiled by the group leaders.

We cannot base the comparison on average rank scores
(cumulative score given to an item by the group divided by the
number of voters in the group), if the members of any one group
picked a different number of finalist items to rank than the
members of any other group, because of the difference in the
number of points allocated by the voters.

Table 3 is based on standard score computations and
permits us to convert average rank scores from each group to
standard score equivalents which can be compared. The procedure
for conversion is as follows:

1. Convert each item score, group by group, to an average rank
    score, by dividing it by the number of voters. Note the number
    of finalist items that each group was asked to rank.
2. Look at the top of the table for the number of finalist items
    that the first group used. In the column below that number,
    locate each item's average rank score and record by it the
    standard score equivalent (at the far left) that corresponds with
    it.
3. Rank the items from the different groups on the basis of the
    standard score equivalents: the higher the equivalent score, the
    more important the rank of the item.

Table 3. Converting Average Rank Scores to Standard Score Equivalents.

Standard Score Equivalents	Average Rank Scores (item score/total voters) (Use column headed by number that matches number of finalist items ranked)							
	10	9	8	7	6	5	4	3
127	10.							
126		9.						
125			8.					
124				7.				
123	9.75							
122		8.75			6.			
121								
120	9.5		7.75			5.		
119				6.75				
118		8.5					4.	
117								
116	9.25		7.50					
116					5.75			
115								
114		8.25		6.50				
113	9.					4.75		3.
112			7.25					
111								
110		8.			5.50			
109	8.75			6.25			3.75	
108		7.						
107								
106	8.50	7.75				4.50		
105					5.25			
104				6.				
103			6.75					
102	8.25	7.50						
101								
100							3.50	2.75
99	8.	7.25	6.50	5.75	5.	4.25		
98								
97								
96								
95	7.75	7.						
94			6.25					
93				5.50				
93					4.75			
92	7.50					4.		
91		6.75					3.25	
90			6.					
89				5.25				
88	7.25							2.50

Table 3. Converting Average Rank Scores to Standard Score Equivalents, Cont'd.

Standard Score Equivalents	Average Rank Scores (item score/total voters) (Use column headed by number that matches number of finalist items ranked)							
	10	9	8	7	6	5	4	3
87		6.50			4.50			
86			5.75					
85	7.					3.75		
84		6.25		5.				
83								
82			5.50		4.25		3.	
81	6.75							
80		6.						
79				4.75				
78	6.50					3.50		
77			5.25					
76		5.75			4.			2.25
75								
74	6.25			4.50				
73			5.				2.75	
72		5.50						
71	6.					3.25		
70					3.75			
69			4.75	4.25				
68	5.75	5.25						
67								
66								
65								
64	5.50	5.	4.50	4.	3.50	3.	2.50	2.
63								
62								
61								
60	5.25	4.75						
59			4.25	3.75				
58					3.25			
57	5.					2.75		
56		4.50						
55			4.				2.25	
54				3.50				
53	4.75							
52		4.25			3.			
51								1.75
50	4.50		3.75			2.50		
49				3.25				

Table 3. Converting Average Rank Scores to Standard Score Equivalents, Cont'd.

Standard Score Equivalents	Average Rank Scores (item score/total voters) (Use column headed by number that matches number of finalist items ranked)							
	10	9	8	7	6	5	4	3
48		4.						
47	4.25							
46			3.50		2.75		2.	
45								
44		3.75		3.				
43	4.					2.25		
42			3.25					
41								
40		3.50			2.50			
39	3.75			2.75				1.50
38			3.					
37		3.25					1.75	
36	3.50					2.		
35					2.25			
34				2.50				
33		3.	2.75					
32	3.25							
31								
30								
29	3.	2.75	2.50	2.25	2.	1.75		
28							1.50	
27								1.25
26	2.75	2.50						
25			2.25					
24				2.				
23					1.75			
22	2.50	2.25				1.50		
21								
20			2.					
19				1.75			1.25	
18	2.25	2.						
17					1.50			
16								
15	2.		1.75			1.25		1.
14		1.75		1.50				
13								
12					1.25			
11	1.75		1.50					
10		1.50					1.	

Table 3. Converting Average Rank Scores to Standard Score Equivalents, Cont'd.

Standard Score Equivalents	Average Rank Scores (item score/total voters) (Use column headed by number that matches number of finalist items ranked)							
	10	9	8	7	6	5	4	3
9				1.25				
8	1.50					1.		
7			1.25					
6		1.25			1.			
5	1.25							
4				1.				
3			1.					
2		1.						
1	1.							

Sample Problem

Suppose we want to compare the final voting results for the following three groups who independently considered the topic: "What are the problems confronting the whole organization?"

Items for:	Voting Tally Score	Average Rank Score	Standard Score Equivalent (from Table 3)
Group A (15 members) 4 finalist items ranked			
6A	55	3.67	106
10A	48	3.20	90
22A	32	2.13	50
2A	15	1.	10
Group B (10 members) 8 finalist items ranked			
7B	68	6.8	104.5
1B	61	6.1	90

42B	50	5.	73
13B	48	4.8	69
3B	38	3.8	51
21B	35	3.5	46
8B	35	3.5	46
4B	25	2.5	29

Group C (20 members)
5 finalist items ranked

2C	91	4.55	108
10C	85	4.25	99
22C	61	3.05	66
13C	43	2.15	41
16C	20	1.	8

The relative importance given to similar or dissimilar problems by the groups can be determined on the basis of standard score equivalents. In the example above, item 2C (of group C) received the highest score (108); 6A (of group A) received the next highest (106); and so on.

Chapter Eight

The Document
Review Meeting

On occasion, a problem should be assigned to a special task force, due to its complexity or to provide the benefit of a special research effort. Then, a document review meeting can be held at which all who have a stake in the solution consider how to improve upon what has been produced.

Other occasions may warrant a document review meeting, such as (1) a supervisor wants his or her group to review a proposed budget or a plan handed down from above; (2) a higher authority needs to check the feasibility of an interagency proposal developed by representatives of several groups; or (3) the time arises for a periodic review of existing rules, policies, and procedures to see if they are still appropriate or can be improved upon. Basically, we use the Improved Nominal Group Technique (INGT) presented in previous chapters, but with the important changes discussed below.

Premeeting Steps

Distribute the document to be reviewed to participants in advance and indicate the purpose of the meeting with a question such as "How can we improve upon this?" Follow this up with a request: "Also, please identify problems which need to be dealt with, even though you have no solutions to offer for them." In preparing the list of anonymous inputs for distribution, it is useful to present perceived problems with the document in a separate section from proposed changes, since dealing with problems will be a separate activity for the group.

Collection and Display Steps

If one or more participants brought completed cards to input, the leader starts the meeting with a card collection round; otherwise, he or she begins with a silent writing period. The same procedures are followed for transcribing inputs to flipchart pages and for handling no-discussion proposals for change, but perceived problems should be transcribed on pages separate from those devoted to proposed changes.

Serial Discussion

The discussion phase is the same as for INGT, except for one important distinction. When the discussion of a proposed change is finished, the leader says: "Is there any objection to the adoption of this change?" If there is no objection, the change is adopted and entered on every participant's copy of the document under review before going to the next item. This facilitates group process and makes voting at the end more manageable.

During the meeting, participants may wish to input additional changes verbally, rather than anonymously. If the changes are brief and do not require discussion, there is no need to record them on the flipchart, unless there is an objection to their adoption. When objections arise, the changes in question should be recorded for later voting.

Voting

When the opportunity has been provided to discuss and adopt all inputs, we are left with perceived problems with the document, and proposed changes which met with one or more objections from the group.

There is no need to ask for a vote on problems that obviously demand attention. Problem-solving meetings may be scheduled for some of them. For others, committees or expert individuals may be asked to write up solution proposals to present to future document review meetings.

Those concerns which are not clearly problems are submitted to an anonymous vote. On 3 x 5 cards, participants indicate by number only those problem items they feel are real problems. They then rank them, assigning the highest value (equal to the number of items to be ranked) to the most important problem, one number lower to the next most important, and so on.

Disposition of any proposed changes that were not adopted due to one or more objections is easy: each is decided upon by anonymous majority vote. The leader requests that each participant list the numbers of the proposed changes on a 3 x 5 card, write *yes* or *no* by each number, and then input the card facedown to a central pile.

Example from Practice. The head of a large division of an air force base was disappointed with his civilian monetary awards program, which involved quality salary increases and sustained superior performance awards. Widespread employee ignorance, general apathy about the program despite repeated publicizing efforts, and criticism of the award process for lack of employee involvement prompted him to seek means for strengthening the awards program.

In response to the author's recommendation, several groups, comprised of representative professional, technical, and clerical employees, were formed to address the question, "How can the present awards system be improved upon?" in document review meetings. Output from the groups made it clear that minor refinements to the existing program would not suffice. There was a definite need for substantial employee involvement in the awards process, but it was not clear how this should be accomplished.

Consequently, a committee was formed to build upon the ideas obtained by soliciting additional ideas and translating them into a proposed plan. The resulting plan called for each subunit head to establish a *peer evaluation board* of three to nine employees to serve in an advisory capacity, each board being free to develop its own evaluation criteria, criteria weights, and format for inputting information. The plan also dealt with issues of eligibility, right of appeal, and related matters. It was submitted to unit document review meetings; minor changes were made; and it was implemented throughout the division.

As might be expected, the first year's experience turned up problems, but every unit wanted to retain the peer board mechanism. Refinements were made on the basis of anonymous responses to the question, "How can this be improved upon?" and the program was judged to be a solid success by all units the second year, with high levels of employee involvement and approval.

Chapter Nine

Program Planning and Other Multiple Group Situations

The Improved Nominal Group Technique (INGT) works well with a single group of up to twenty participants. To accommodate more people, we create two or more groups to work on the same assignment simultaneously, each with its own leader, flipcharts, etc.

Each group follows the same INGT procedures presented in previous chapters for a single group. Then, the leaders meet to determine which of their groups' finalist items are basically similar.

Meeting of Leaders

INGT is *not* used for the meeting of group leaders. The meeting starts with each leader listing his or her group's finalist items on a flipchart page for display.

Items that appear to be basically similar in intent or meaning, despite different wording, are discussed by the leaders of the groups which produced them. If there is agreement that the

Note: The general rationale for this chapter (and, in particular, the types of information to solicit during premeeting activity) draw heavily upon Delbecq, Van de Ven, and Gustafson (1975) and Delbecq and Van de Ven (1971).

items *are* similar, rewording may be used to highlight the similarity of meaning that the respective groups had in mind.

One leader's objection, however, is all that is required to block the rewording or assumed similarity of any items. These will be retained as separate finalist items for presentation at a *consolidated meeting* of all participants.

The meeting of group leaders ends with the production of a *consolidated list* of finalist items in which there are no unanimously acknowledged duplications. Typically, a number of items will have been judged similar, and several of these will have been slightly reworded.

> *Examples from Practice.* In each of the earlier examples from practice that involved multiple groups, the leaders met after their groups finished the INGT process to produce a consolidated list of finalist items for consideration by all group members meeting together: the four university hospital leaders who took part in a retreat (described on page 46), the six leaders who conducted flextime review sessions (described on pages 71–72), and the many leaders who conducted several waves of document review meetings associated with the development and refinement of a new monetary awards program (described on pages 80–81).
>
> In every instance these meetings went well, the leaders experiencing little difficulty in agreeing about the disposition of finalist items. During only one of the *consolidated meetings* of all participants did a group member challenge the melding of one of his group's items with another. As a result, it was unmelded and again listed separately.

Consolidated Meeting

The first step at the consolidated meeting of all participants is for one of the leaders to present the consolidated list of finalist items to the participants, indicating which of the items represent acknowledged duplications.

If, after hearing explanations from the leaders involved, any participant objects to the handling of any item, that item should be reestablished on the consolidated list in the form in which it was taken to the meeting of the leaders.

When there are no further questions about duplicate or reworded items, the presiding leader initiates *serial discussion* of the items on the final form of the consolidated list. He or she provides participants with the opportunity to ask for clarification about the meaning of an item and the opportunity to speak for or against it, giving their reasons if they wish. At any time, a participant may propose to reword, combine, or eliminate items on display; however, only one objection will block the change with no explanation required. In other words, the discussion is conducted according to the INGT guidelines.

However, proposals to add new items to the consolidated list are not permitted, because the finalist items on display represent high-priority group concerns rather than individual ones. Presumably, individual concerns were given a fair chance to make the finalist list in the INGT group meetings. When serial discussion of the items on the consolidated list ends, and there are no more proposals for changing them, it is time for the *first vote*.

Voting follows the procedures outlined in Chapter Eight. The presiding leader asks each participant to indicate and rank order (on a 3 x 5 card) a prescribed number of most important items from the finalist list. If the tally of the voting indicates a high level of inconsistency or many equally valued items, it may be useful to repeat the serial discussion of these indecisively chosen items in preparation for a *second vote* on them. The emerging top priority items represent the preferences of all participants from all of the groups, acting in concert.

Program Planning

In planning a community-wide or organization-wide program that will involve different client, consumer, or interest groups, we find that the problems associated with conventional group problem-solving methods become even more pronounced. Some established administrators and professionals will defend existing approaches, other influentials will try to displace objective evidence with emotional appeals, and many nonprofessional, rank-and-file stakeholders will feel intimidated and ineffectual.

When INGT is added to sound program-planning procedure, these and other threats to effective problem identification and problem solving can be minimized or eliminated.

Defining Problems or Needs. Delbecq, Van de Ven, and Gustafson (1975) report: "In our experience, professionals are always sure they 'know' what the problems of consumers are. However, in every instance when we asked consumers to indicate their priority concerns, there has been a significant difference in the concerns identified by them as compared to the concerns listed by professionals . . . they perceive problems from a different perspective than do consumers" (p. 121).

The use of INGT's anonymous inputting procedure by representatives of the various groups helps to play down mere window dressing and to focus upon real need and problem areas. For example, suppose we want to explore ways to improve the functioning of a city's government. First, we should form problem-identification groups to represent every constituency: the various government departments and the various youth and adult consumer groups of present or potential services.

Next, we ask participants to deposit their anonymous input in conveniently located boxes before a stated deadline, the question(s) posed to them specific to the purpose of the program. We might ask of participants: "Please list all of the problems that you feel currently interfere with our functioning or with our more effectively serving you."

Or we might request answers to the following questions: (1) What are the needs you feel this agency should serve? (2) Please indicate by each need whether the agency meets it, only partly meets it, or doesn't meet it at all. (3) What reasons do you feel account for why the agency is not adequately meeting this (specify) need?

Before deciding upon the final form or wording that the question(s) should take, run a check on perceived meaning by asking several typical participants how they would interpret the question(s).

After the premeeting steps (outlined on pages 43, 48) are satisfied, the remaining parts of the INGT process (pages 49–66, 70) are completed by each problem-identification group.

Next, the leaders of the groups meet to develop a consolidated list of finalist items to present to a mass meeting of all participants, following the procedure presented in the first part of this chapter.

Creating Problem-Solving Groups. The list of finalist needs or problems that results from the mass meeting of problem-identification participants should be classified into appropriate categories.

A primary breakdown might be on the basis of agency or organizational subunit jurisdiction. A secondary breakdown might then be made on the basis of the technical characteristics of the need or problem areas.

The purpose of this classification is to guide the formation of problem-solving groups to deal with each set of needs or problems. For example, one of the primary categories for the items collected in connection with the program for improving city government might be Law Enforcement.

A secondary breakdown of items under Law Enforcement might produce headings such as Community-Police Relations, Recruitment and Training of Law Enforcement Officers, and Crime Prevention.

Problem-solving groups for these categories should be designed to involve appropriate specialist personnel as well as representatives of various community law enforcement groups and related administrative groups.

It is useful to use a chart, like the one shown in Figure 7, for keeping track of individuals who should be invited to participate or should be kept informed of developments.

The name of each person to be contacted is shown on a horizontal line, and each need or problem area is given a vertical

Figure 7. Name: Problems or Needs Chart.

Problem or Need Area

| Name, Address, Phone | Law Enforcement | | |
	Community Relations	*Recruiting, Training*	*Crime Prevention*
Ms. Jane Doe 1770 Oak St., 32601 377-4332	I, S	NP	NP
Dr. Ralph Trixler 836 Main, 32611 376-8664	NP	A, S, M	NP
Mr. Don Brown (Ret.) 1015 Main St, 32611 376-3442	I, R	NP	I, R
Sgt. William Wolfe Police Dept. 378-6642	NP	NP	S, M

Code: A = administrator who has authority to approve or veto plans/action for topic; M = will be involved in plan implementation; I = influential person interested in this topic; R = representative of an affected or interested group for this topic; S = person with special knowledge or experience relating to this topic; NP = person will not attend meetings for topic, but should be kept informed about developments.

column. The appropriate code letter (or letters if an individual represents more than one category) is placed in the box made by the vertical and horizontal columns.

Of course, the code we use should be adapted to our particular needs. Its sole purpose is to suggest who should be invited to join each problem-solving group and who should be kept informed of developments with regard to the solution of each type of problem. Oversights in this regard can deny us valuable inputs and create unnecessary opposition to the implementation of solutions.

Premeeting Activity. Before actually meeting, the members of each problem-solving group should be given a list of the need and/or problem areas (as provided by classification of the final output of the mass meeting of problem-identification participants) they are to address; and, they should be asked to respond to the following questions through premeeting, anonymous inputting.

- Which of the problems or needs can be satisfied with existing resources? Please explain how.
- Which of the problems or needs will require new resources? Please indicate what kind(s) by each, and be as specific as you can.
- What additional resource people should be invited to participate in our deliberations? Please explain your choices.
- What literature should be reviewed in preparation for our deliberations? Please identify materials fully.

While obtaining responses to these questions from each group member, it is useful to solicit responses from all interested parties in the organization or community at the same time. This can be accomplished via publication of the finalist list of need and problem areas, along with the above list of questions and the invitation to respond, in a house organ or newspaper.

Through this approach, we can encourage a grassroots understanding and support for the program. We can also obtain valuable additional information and, at the same time, uncover out-of-group apprehensions or objections early enough to deal with them effectively.

Document Review Meetings. The problem-solving groups may find it useful to ask highly qualified individuals or subgroups to prepare detailed written proposals for dealing with specific issues, their written proposals to be reviewed at subsequent document review meetings using the procedure presented in Chapter Eight.

The document review meeting, coupled with the multiple group procedure presented at the beginning of this chapter, provides an excellent coordinated approach when several groups must evaluate a plan, budget, or proposal that originated elsewhere but affects them all.

Each group conducts its own document review meeting to review and refine the materials. Then, the leaders of the groups meet to meld the changes and refinements proposed by their respective groups for subsequent consideration by all participants in a consolidated meeting.

Multiple Criteria. Sometimes, there is no clearly correct standard for choosing from among alternatives. For example, in guiding decisions for a community development program, a standard of social desirability may produce a result quite different than would a standard of technical desirability.

It may be wise to use more than one standard in the decision-making process in such situations. This is illustrated by the case of a police department that wanted to use hollow-point ammunition, which flattens on impact. The department claimed that such ammunition would provide greater stopping power, would inflict less injury, and would be less likely to ricochet and possibly injure bystanders than the solid bullets in use. However, minority groups and the American Civil Liberties Union challenged these claims and opposed the change. The controversy was resolved by recognizing and dealing with two separate issues: technical considerations and social values.

Ballistics experts were asked to evaluate various combinations of bullet type and powder charge in terms of degree of injury, stopping power, and threat to bystanders, while policy makers and special interest group representatives made judgments about the social acceptability of various levels of these factors.

It was agreed that the three factors should receive equal weight for each type of evaluation—technical desirability and social acceptability—and, in turn, that the two types of evaluation should be equally weighted.

The result was the selection of a bullet that had greater stopping power than the one in use, but one that was less likely to cause injury than the hollow-point type originally requested (Hammond and Adelman, 1976).

Representatives should agree first on the various standards to use, related subcriteria, and the relative weights to assign to them. INGT provides an excellent means for making these decisions, starting with anonymous premeeting inputting. The results are used to guide subsequent selection of priority items and the modification of written proposals through participant voting in each group. Last, final group results guide deliberation in the consolidated meeting of all participants.

Gaining Acceptance. The strengths of the Improved Nominal Group Technique help ensure understanding and acceptance of the decisions made. What can we do to gain the support of nonparticipants who are in a position to either obstruct or facilitate the implementation of our program? Compared to participants, they are usually less informed about our planning and less appreciative of its quality. Typically, they have a strong emotional or material stake in maintaining the status quo.

The premeeting input distribution sheets and flipchart pages from the various INGT meetings provide invaluable tools for briefing nonparticipants. When these are displayed and interpreted by group leaders, key elements of each group's decision-making process can be recreated from beginning to end: the total array of items considered, those eliminated, the nature of changes made to others, and the votes received by all. These are matters of record, not conjecture or selective recall.

It is difficult for a nonparticipant to leave such a briefing with any false impressions that important alternatives were ignored or that the final outcome was not truly representative of the participants. The Name: Problems or Needs Chart (Figure 7) helps us to avoid overlooking key nonparticipants who should receive such briefing.

Another tool for gaining understanding and commitment is the Risk Description Technique (Maier and Verser, 1982). A document review meeting is scheduled for objectors to the program plan as well as its supporters. Prior to the meeting, anonymous premeeting responses are solicited from objectors to the question: "What dangers or risks do you see in the proposed program?" The input is then duplicated and distributed to the participants and to the leaders of the groups who developed or reviewed the program. The group leaders should be at the meeting to respond to the fears and objections revealed.

When the meeting reaches the first vote stage, instructions should be "List up to X number of items that you feel are important dangers or risks (X equals 15 percent of the number of still active items on display) and rank them (most important receives value X, next most important value X minus 1, and so on). If you feel that no item constitutes an important risk or danger, write 'none' on your 3 x 5 card."

Most concerns will be disposed of during the serial discussion phase of the meeting through a ventilation of feelings and the clarification provided by the leaders from the various groups. However, those dangers or risks which do show up as finalist items through the voting process should be dealt with in subsequent INGT problem-solving meetings or document review meetings held to evaluate proposed solutions.

For opponents who appear to be quite knowledgeable about the program plan and claim to be sympathetic with its goals, an INGT meeting might be arranged to present them with the question: "How can we improve upon this plan?" If they cannot come up with solid objections or constructive alternatives, it will be difficult for them to continue their opposition, at least publicly.

Example from Practice. The development of a new monetary awards program, an earlier example from practice, also serves as an illustration of program planning. After reviewing the performance of all eligible personnel, the existing program called for immediate supervisors to complete resumes for those they wished to nominate for an award, citing specific reasons. Final selections were made by an awards board comprised of the heads of the various division units. Unfortunately, the program had never generated much employee interest or enthusiasm. Many were poorly informed about it, despite repeated publicity campaigns, and others were skeptical about the objectivity of the evaluation process.

Management decided to invite employee representatives from each unit to participate in the development of a more effective program. They were formed into six groups to deal with the question: "How can the present awards program be improved upon?" Meetings were conducted on the basis of this book's procedures, coupled with the multigroup procedures described in this chapter.

The top-rated items that came out of the final, secret votes of each group were integrated into a proposed operating plan by a committee of group leaders. In turn, this plan was submitted to document review meetings of the six groups with the question: "How can we improve upon this proposal?" The resulting finished plan provided for the establishment of a Peer Evaluation Board in each unit to solicit and process nominations and to submit recommendations, with supporting documentation, to the unit head. The new program worked well. The top recommendations of the peer boards were accepted, and employees displayed high levels of interest and confidence in the awards process and its results.

Chapter Ten

Putting It All Together:
An Overview of the Process

Each guideline presented in the preceding chapters has proven effective in its own right. When we put these guidelines together, we have the best approach yet developed for problem-free problem solving. It's called Improved Nominal Group Technique, or INGT, a refinement of Nominal Group Technique (NGT), developed by Delbecq, Van de Ven, and Gustafson (1975) on the basis of extensive research.

The Improved Nominal Group Technique comprises the Nominal Group Technique with the following improvements.

- NGT makes no provision for the inputting and review of ideas from participants *before* a meeting. INGT draws upon the proven Delphi technique (Dalkey and Helmer, 1963) to add productive, premeeting activity.
- NGT uses the verbal inputting of ideas. This compromises the NGT ideal of anonymous authorship. INGT satisfies this ideal through the use of 3 x 5 cards.
- NGT permits only one person to input since only one person transcribes the input at any given time. This can create a bottleneck, and it sets a group size limit of nine participants for effective operation. With card inputting, INGT permits simultaneous inputting by all and simultaneous transcription by as many as are needed. We have had successful meetings with up to twenty participants.

- NGT provides for the review of a proposal only in its preliminary, outline form. INGT develops this concept to provide for the premeeting, as well as in-meeting, review of finished rules, policies, procedures, budgets, plans, proposals, charters, or any other documents in a document review meeting.

The basic steps of INGT and the reasons for using them were discussed in Chapters Three through Seven. A recap is presented below.

Summary of Premeeting Steps

1. Determine the purpose of the meeting carefully:

- Be sure the problems you have identified are the real ones by having a problem-identification meeting with anonymous inputting.
- If a problem-solving meeting is called, do participants know what characteristics an acceptable solution must have? Do they know those characteristics which, if improved beyond the required level, will improve the value of a solution? If not, this information should be developed and distributed beforehand.
- Do not attempt too much in one meeting. Schedule a single-purpose meeting for each of the following:
  - Identifying and prioritizing problems, positions, or options.
  - Solving a specific problem.
  - Reviewing a written proposal or other document. (Steps for this type of meeting are presented in Chapter Eight.)

2. Communicate the purpose to participants in advance. Request that they anonymously submit written ideas on 3 x 5 cards to be dropped in a conveniently placed box by a deadline that allows enough premeeting time for step 3.

3. After the deadline, number and list each submitted idea without change. Duplicate the list and distribute it to participants with the following instructions: "Please jot down and bring to the

meeting any proposals you want to make for changing the wording of any item or for combining any items. Also, write any additional items on 3 x 5 cards to input, anonymously, at the beginning of the meeting.''

Note: Even if lack of time prevents completing steps 2 and 3 above, announce the purpose of the meeting in advance—if no more than the day before—so that participants may complete cards to input in an initial card collection round.

4. Arrange for necessary supplies to be on hand and necessary equipment to be set up in a suitable room (details presented in Chapter Four).

Summary of Collection and Display Steps

1. If INGT is new to some participants, the leader gives a brief overview of how it operates, stressing the importance of observing the rules. (Presumably, those unfamiliar with the approach were given information about INGT well in advance of the meeting.)

If a premeeting list of inputs was duplicated and distributed, the leader makes a copy available to anyone who did not bring his list to the meeting.

2. If one or more participants brought completed input cards to the meeting, the leader conducts a card collection round:

Leader: Since some of you have brought completed cards with you let's start with a card collection round. Everyone please put a card face down in the center of the table for me to collect. If you don't have a card with an idea on it right now, submit a blank one face down. This assures everyone's anonymity.

When all cards are in the pile, the leader mixes them around before picking them up, sorts out the blank ones for reuse, and sees how many items there are to transcribe to flipchart pages. If there are more than five or six items, the leader shares the cards with others so they can be transcribed quickly to the several flipcharts available. To distinguish the items, one transcriber can put *A* after each of his or her item's numbers, another can use *B*, and so on. As each flipchart page is filled with inputs, it is attached to the wall with masking tape where everyone can see it.

3. The leader announces a silent writing period:

Leader (while distributing several blank 3 x 5 cards to each participant, leaving a reserve pile of cards on the table): Our procedure calls for inputting your ideas anonymously and displaying them before we discuss the pros and cons of any of them. We'll have a five to ten minute silent writing period now to prepare cards for another collection round. See if the items going up on display suggest additional ones to you. You can put as many items as you wish on one card, just try to be concise and specific. Remember: Don't identify yourself.

The leader performs or oversees the transcription and display of items from the cards to flipchart pages, while observing the writing activity of participants to determine when another card collection round will be appropriate. (The silent writing/card collection round/transcription and display routine is continued until a card collection round produces all blank cards.)

4. At any time any participant is permitted to propose the rewording of an item, the combination of interdependent items, or the elimination of apparently duplicate items. The leader lets the group know that such no-discussion proposals for change may be made, but does not call for them or promote them in any way. An item should not be eliminated because someone does not like it, nor should items be combined just for the sake of consolidation. We do not want to restrict voting options unduly.

Leader: It is proposed that such and such be done (repeating exactly what was proposed). Is there any objection?

If one hand goes up, the change is blocked. No explanation is required, although the objector is free to volunteer one. The matter is not debatable, nor subject to majority vote. Changes are noted on the flipchart or by the items affected at the time the changes are accepted.

5. When the last card collection round produces all blank cards, and all items are on display, it is time to move to the serial discussion phase of the meeting:

Leader: We're ready now to move into the discussion phase of our meeting, since all of the cards in the last collection round were blank. However, this does not close the door on making no-discussion proposals for change or on inputting new items. You can submit new items verbally or in writing at any time during our discussion phase. However, if you prefer to input through another card collection round, let me know and I'll conduct one.

Summary of Serial Discussion Steps

1. The leader goes through the entire list of items, inviting comment item by item before voting takes place. If the number of items poses a problem in relation to the time remaining for the present meeting, the leader should determine the group's wishes. Can the present meeting be extended? Can an additional meeting be scheduled? Should a time limit be set for the discussion of any one item? The decision should be determined by majority vote.

2. The leader reminds the group of the following additional guidelines, enforcement of which is the leader's responsibility.

- The discussion phase is for seeking or giving clarification about meaning and for speaking for or against an item. It is *not* for arguments, unsolicited repetition of a point, or attempts to reach agreement about each item. However, participants may seek explanation from a presenter about how his or her ideas would deal with a particular need or difficulty.
- There is no obligation for participants to discuss any item, only the assured opportunity to do so.
- At any time, a participant can return to an item presented earlier for further discussion, provided that the total discussion time for that item does not exceed any agreed-upon limit.

Leader (continuing): If there are no questions about procedure, let's start the serial discussion. (Leader refers to item #1 on the premeeting distribution list, if there is one; otherwise, he points to the first item on display on the wall and reads it aloud to the group.) Any comment on #1?

Group member: Yes, it says the problem is inadequate communications. Just what does that mean? Communication with whom? And by whom?

Leader: We have a request for clarification of #1. Anyone care to respond? The fact that you do won't necessarily mean it's your item. In fact, we don't want to know whose item it is, unless the author wants us to know.

Another group member: Well, it's not mine, but what it means to me is that we are not kept adequately informed about developments outside of our group which affect our work. I propose changing item #1 to say just that.

Leader: We have a proposal to change #1, "Inadequate communications," to "Not kept adequately informed about developments outside of our group which affect our work." Is there any objection to this change? (Waiting and seeing no hand go up, the leader draws a light line through "Inadequate communications," or asks participants to draw a line through it if they've received a premeeting distribution list that includes this item. In either case, the new wording is written below the item or at the end of the list if there is not enough space, and it is still identified as item #1.) Any further discussion of #1 as it now stands? (One person describes how it affects his particular job. Another describes the frustration of being in the dark.)

Leader (seeing no more hands raised, moves to the next item): Any comment on #2, "Assignment of overtime work is unfair to newcomers"?

And so it goes, until the group has had the opportunity to discuss all items. The leader functions as a facilitator of productive group action by enforcing the rules and guidelines.

Having transcribed any last minute items onto the flipchart, provided the group with opportunity to discuss them, and processed any further no-discussion proposals for change, the leader announces that the group is ready for the first vote.

Summary of Voting Steps

1. If the purpose of the meeting is to identify problems, the question for the first vote is "What are the X (X equals 15 percent of the total number of items on display) most important items (problems)?"

Leader: Select your X (specify the appropriate number) items without consulting anyone. We want your private, independent vote. If you have difficulty in reading any of the sheets on display, feel free to get up and move closer to them. Consider all items before making your selection. Then, put the item number of the X (again specify number) you have selected on a 3 x 5 card, which will be your ballot. Next, rank each selection by placing a circled number next to each item. Give the most important item the highest rank, which in this case is equal to X (same number). Give the next most important item a rank number one less than that, and so on. Circling your rank numbers helps us to avoid confusing them with your item numbers when we tally the results. (At this point, the leader may wish to put a sample ballot on a flipchart and recommend use of the alternation ranking technique; see Chapter Seven for details.) When you have completed your ballot, please turn it over and put it in a pile in the center of the table so that we can assure voting anonymity.

When a large number of items is being voted upon, participants may wish to classify the items before voting. One possibility might be problems which can be solved by our group; problems which must be solved through collaboration with people outside of our group; and problems which must be solved by others, who may or may not decide to solicit our advice. Participants then vote on the three to five most important items in each category.

If the purpose of the meeting is to solve a problem, the question for the first vote is "Which of these solutions are acceptable to you?" The leader would instruct participants to list the item numbers of up to three solutions in order of perceived importance, placing the most important at the top of the list.

From these results, two or three finalist solutions are identified. As an alternative to another ranking, participants can enter their item numbers on a 3 x 5 card and write *yes* or *no* by each. They then submit the cards facedown, to a pile in the center of the table. The solution that receives the most *yes* votes (equal to at least 51 percent of the number of voters) is the winner. (If ties are permitted, see details for handling them in Chapter Seven.)

2. When all face down ballots are in, the leader mixes them around before picking them up to assure anonymity for the last ballots on the pile. Next, with the help of a group member, the leader tallies the rank values assigned to each item. One person can dictate as the other writes the rank values by item numbers displayed on a flipchart page (see Figure 5). In most cases, the first vote will produce five or six items that stand apart, having significantly higher scores than the other items. When this happens, the first vote is the final vote. However, there are times when the results of the first vote raise doubts (see pages 65–66). In such cases, a second vote may be needed.

3. If there is evidence to suggest that a second vote may be useful, the leader should place the matter before the group:

Leader (noting the number of clustered items on the tally below the two or three clear-cut winners and/or noting the variation in rank values assigned to the same items):   If the group is willing, we'll probably benefit from reopening discussion on these items. Then we'll have a second vote to determine which items to add to the clear-cut winners from the first vote.

Assuming the group agrees, the leader reopens discussion on the items in question, accepting new items and no-discussion proposals for change as done previously. The second vote is conducted and tallied in the same way as the first vote. Except, if there are only five or six finalist items, it may be useful to have participants rank all of them to determine the next most important items to add below the two or three clear-cut winners from the first vote. (See Chapter Seven for details on how to adjust voting results for intergroup comparisons.)

4. If the purpose of the meeting is problem identification and the group did not classify problems before voting took place (see middle of page 60), it may be useful now to classify winning items into appropriate categories to facilitate planning for future action. In addition, it may be useful to decide which problems in each category require action most urgently. Thus, we set the stage for deciding whether our group should meet as a whole to solve a particular problem or whether we should charge a committee with developing a proposed solution to submit to a document review meeting (see Chapter Eight).

5. Before leaving, the leader sees that all displayed flipchart pages are placed together (after the adhesive ends of masking tape have been folded over or cut off) and rolled up for storage, serving as a permanent record of what took place for refreshing the group in the future and for briefing others.

Important: Before you attempt to conduct your first INGT meeting, be sure to test your understanding of the rules and procedures by taking the test presented at the end of this book.

Chapter Eleven

Management by Objectives

In previous chapters, we have examined ways in which the Improved Nominal Group Technique (INGT) minimizes or overcomes the many barriers that conventional procedures put in the way of unfettered, high-production participation. We have explored the documented advantages of realistically defined purpose, premeeting activity, anonymous inputting, complete input display, postponed evaluation, assured discussion opportunity, research-based discussion guidelines, and the benefits of these elements combined for reviewing completed documents and for program planning and other multiple group situations.

In this and the following two chapters, we will see how these tools can be applied to various specialized programs to revitalize them or to enhance and sustain their success. Here, we will start with *management by objectives* (MBO), a program more often in trouble than not. We will look at key problem areas and discuss the role that INGT can play in dealing with them.

The idea underlying management by objectives is well supported by research findings: specific, hard goals that are understood and accepted improve performance, compared to conditions in which we have one or more of these factors missing (Miner, 1980). However, there is one problem: MBO usually goes awry in organizations when applied on an individualistic, one-on-one basis.

Perceived Speed-Up

Under MBO, the goals of subordinates are supposed to be set participatively, not by coercive arm twisting. Presumably, if a subordinate does a good job, he or she will have the option of aiming for the same performance in the future. Rarely, in actual practice, is this choice available at lower levels. Managers commit their units to increased output, then present this to subordinates as a given. The only thing for them to collaborate on is the question of how to do it.

More often than not, employees resent this approach. They may see different areas in need of improvement, or they may feel the need to catch their breath, rather than move ahead immediately. Even if employees agree upon the same areas, they may choose a different amount of improvement to shoot for, depending upon the perceived rewards for increased performance.

Is it any wonder that many employees react negatively in organization after organization as they come to see MBO as nothing more than the old-fashioned "speed-up" in new packaging.

Teamwork "Down the Tube"

Even when collaborative, one-on-one goal-setting is present under MBO, another problem emerges. Quantifiable, egoistic goals start to take over the ballgame. Team-oriented activity and less quantifiable goals, such as helping others and taking advantage of unforeseen opportunities, receive less and less attention. As concern grows about optimizing personal gain irrespective of the organization's larger needs, the spirit of collaborative purpose and effort begins to go down the tube.

Clearly, this is *not* the direction in which an organization should move. A meta-analysis of 122 studies shows that cooperation promotes higher achievement than does individualistic effort, both with and without intergroup competition (Johnson, Maruyama, Johnson, and Nelson, 1981).

And a recent study of sixty-two prominent companies in the United States produced a similar finding. In looking for the characteristics that distinguish the best performers over a twenty-year period, Peters and Waterman report that "Small groups are, quite simply, the basic organizational building blocks of excellent companies" (1982, p. 126).

Need for Group Involvement

The solution indicated by these findings and those of others, such as Rensis Likert (1973), is the formal addition of the group concept to an MBO program, to yield Management by Group Objectives (MBGO). Each subordinate participates in setting team objectives, as well as his or her own objectives.

To create the right climate for good goal setting, each group should also periodically review the rules, policies, procedures, and other constraints under which goal-setting and related activities must operate to see if they need to be changed.

Role of INGT

The Improved Nominal Group Technique (summarized in Chapter Ten) provides an excellent means of introducing Management by Group Objectives. It minimizes the need for experience in group leadership and it conserves valuable group time.

Overall organizational objectives should be based upon a realistic appraisal of personnel strengths and other organizational resources in relation to external needs and demands.

Whenever possible, objectives should also be congruent with what Ackoff (1970) refers to as the "stylistic objectives" of the management team. He feels that by making explicit our emotion-based preferences about what the organization should and should not be doing (without regard to current tests of profitability), we can clear the air for more consistent and enthusiastic pursuit of goals which satisfy *both* considerations.

According to Peters and Waterman, the use of this approach is a key reason for the top performance of our leading companies: "The top performers create a broad, uplifting, shared culture, a coherent framework within which charged-up people search for appropriate adaptations. Their ability to extract extraordinary contributions from very large numbers of people turns on the ability to create a sense of highly valued purpose. . . . Instead of trying to overcome resistance to what people are *not* ready to do, find out what they *are* ready to do" (1982, pp. 51, 149).

With regard to typical MBO programs, Peters and Waterman go on to suggest that "such high purpose is inherently at odds with 30 quarterly MBO objectives, 25 measures of cost containment, 100 demeaning rules for production-line workers, or an ever changing, analytically derived strategy that stresses costs this year, innovation next, and heaven knows what the year after" (1982, p. 51).

First, we need to get an honest indication of likes and dislikes before we can determine which goals associated with these preferences will meet our other requirements. The premeeting, anonymous inputting phase of INGT provides an excellent means of discerning honest opinion. Questions to stimulate inputting might be "What would you most like to see this organization doing five years from now?" and "What would you least like to see it doing then?"

Next, we need to have a regular INGT meeting to select a subset of key goals from the ideas submitted, taking into account other requirements which must be satisfied.

In addition, it may be desirable to establish certain standing personal goals, whether or not these areas are covered in any individual MBO "contract." Such goals might deal with helping others and taking advantage of unexpected opportunities.

Periodic review of the rules, policies, procedures, and other constraints that goal-setting and related activities must satisfy is needed to see if any of these should be changed. This is more important than most leaders realize. Necessary, up-to-date, and well-conceived rules, policies, and procedures provide a needed curb on the capricious use of power; they give organizational members a perceived freedom in acting; they make the actions and expectations of others more predictable; and they facilitate effective self-guided initiative.

We tend to put off such reviews because we know that they can be very time consuming. True, they can, when we use conventional group procedures. But this is not likely when we use the INGT procedure for document review meetings presented in Chapter Eight.

The addition of MBGO and INGT can breathe new life into an MBO program. And, from time to time, don't forget to hold the most important document review meeting of all: one devoted to the question, "How can we improve upon this MBO/MBGO program?"

Chapter Twelve

Autonomous Work Groups, Quality Circles, Plantwide Incentive Plans, and Other Special Program Groups

It is much easier to visualize the wave of the future than to ride its crest. Why have so many experiments with *autonomous* or *self-managing work groups, employee-employer boards,* and *quality circles* floundered? How can we improve upon the performance of the already largely successful Scanlon, Rucker, Improshare, and Multiple Management plan committees? How can we help managers to have more productive problem-solving meetings as part of a *survey feedback* program? These are the important concerns of this chapter.

Autonomous Work Groups

When a group's work requires coordinated team effort that can be clearly separated from the work of other groups, guiding the group toward a large degree of self-regulation—helping it to become an autonomous work group—can be beneficial to all concerned.

After some carefully developed autonomous work groups proved themselves in England in the 1950s and in Norway in the

1960s, experimentation with work-design innovations became something of a fad in Sweden and elsewhere. With a few notable exceptions, many got on the bandwagon without understanding the requirements for success (Trist, 1981; Thorsrud, 1984). Many employers tried to prescribe a new kind of involvement for traditional workers, failing to realize that productive autonomy is the result of careful planning and nurturing. For example, Tichy and Nisberg (1976) describe the first efforts at Volvo Skodeverken in Sweden, which manufactures gasoline and diesel engines. A predominantly noncollaborative implementation process was used, whereby the "experts" told the workers how to extend their work roles. Hoped-for improvement in absenteeism and turnover did not occur, and workers' reactions were mixed.

Hilgendorf and Irving observe: "Given that participation has to be learned and that the opportunities for learning appear to be unequally distributed in industrial settings because of the way in which the division of labor has been achieved, then the design of participatory schemes must take into account not only that a learning process is involved but the kind of learning which is involved, the unequal opportunity afforded individuals to learn, and the differences between individuals in their learning potential . . . structures should allow different levels of activity by those who achieve different levels of performance" (1976, pp. 503–504).

Even successful autonomous groups are plagued by the inefficiencies of conventional group problem solving. A Swedish corporate director of planning and control observed: "One of the most common complaints about shop-floor democracy is the many hours of nonproductive time spent on discussions" (Arbose, 1979, p. 14). And Simmons and Mares, who have studied many autonomous work groups in America, point out "One of the consultant's most important functions is to teach the new skills of participative management, such as problem-solving skills and the art of conducting a good meeting—basic democratic behavior" (1983, p. 180).

An additional problem stems from the likelihood that the same managers upon whom much of the success of such a program depends will be among the most reluctant agents of change. Simmons and Mares explain why: "Democratization of the workplace threatens first-level supervisors and middle managers more than any other group. For years they have been taught to keep their noses clean and get the production out. Their rewards were promotions, money, prestige, and perhaps a chance to 'kick ass and take names' " (1983, p. 232). Effective shopfloor participation not only undermines the unilateral exercise of power, it forces supervisors and middle managers to adjust to new roles.

Experience at General Motors. Nowhere are the problems that arise from the improper introduction of autonomous work groups, nor the rewards which go with their proper introduction, better illustrated than at General Motors.

According to Tichy and Nisberg (1976), GM's troubles began in 1971 when the company decided to build its new mobile home product with eight six-member teams, four four-member teams, and fourteen three-member teams. Although the team members were handpicked, they apparently had no part in investigating the team approach elsewhere and in planning for its implementation in their shop. They were given no guidance about how teams might organize and coordinate their activities. In addition, existing information and control systems were not reviewed with regard to their suitability for the new setup.

What is most surprising is that Tichy and Nisberg report that no formal procedure existed for periodically reviewing the new program, to turn up problems and to solicit suggestions for improvement. There is little wonder that the team concept slowly died during the next few years.

This type of organization development (OD) work was supposed to give workers some real influence regarding problems and conditions surrounding their work. Yet, when OD was introduced at GM's Lordstown assembly plant, workers dubbed it "overtime and doughnuts," because problems of real concern weren't discussed.

Today, things are different. General Motors has learned the basic lessons well. Now, the front-knuckle and brake-assembly section in the Chevrolet gear and axle plant in Detroit has a nonsynchronized line that workers can start and stop at will. No longer are they chained to a fixed tempo, and every Monday morning volunteers meet in some twenty *quality circles* to participate in the identification and solution of work-related problems. They do so with a big advantage over the early mobile home teams, due to the training in problem-solving techniques they receive (Simmons and Mares, 1983).

An even greater degree of autonomy is being given to workers at certain plants, such as the battery plant in the South where the best labor-management relations and the highest performance levels in the company are being attained. Middle managers act more as resource people than bosses. Workers elect their team leaders, discipline fellow workers, participate in regular team meetings, and are paid on the basis of their level of expertise rather than the current task at hand (Manz and Sims, 1984; Simmons and Mares, 1983).

General Motors, like many organizations today, is extending this highly successful approach to additional units, but only after giving essential preparation, such as training about group process, to unit personnel.

Role of INGT. When autonomous work groups are formed, they are particularly vulnerable to the problems that accompany conventional group problem solving. As one eminent researcher-consultant points out: "For groups to function effectively, individuals need to have both group-process and problem-solving analysis skills. . . . It seems that, particularly in the early history of work teams, considerable supervisory/trainer presence is necessary in order for groups to develop correct norms and skills" (Lawler, 1984, p. 322). They need the opportunities, encouragement, and protection afforded by Improved Nominal Group Technique.

For example, without the anonymous inputting of ideas, many low-status workers may withhold their opinions for fear of appearing foolish to members who are better educated. Others will not say what they think for fear of being punished for voicing negative opinions, regardless of assurances to the contrary. For many of us, trust is established more by actions than by words.

Those who practice traditional, autocratic supervision do not automatically "get religion" when top management commits to a new philosophy. Throughout the hierarchy, it is difficult for the established supervisory and specialist personnel to give up their existing roles, relationships, and prerogatives. INGT's explicit procedures are, in effect, operational guidelines for buiding teams—guidelines that are difficult to subvert once they have been committed to publicly. They provide genuine, self-implementing protection against residual autocratic tendencies to subordinate personnel.

On the other hand, INGT provides the nonautocratic supervisor with an unobtrusive and highly effective tool for achieving her or his primary objective: development of the self-managing capabilities of the group. In weaning the group away from its reliance on his or her direction, the supervisor must avoid providing too little direction as well as too much. The supervisor can achieve this balance through the use of INGT meetings, because INGT procedures nurture *both* growth and achievement at the same time. In addition, by inputting ideas anonymously, the supervisor can give the group the benefit of years of experience without undermining its budding initiative.

Even as autonomous groups grow in experience and feelings of group identification, the need for anonymous inputting by group members remains. The more we come to value our membership in a group, the more we are tempted to evade the truth about the group's needs and problems, out of the fear of embarrassing others or of appearing to be disloyal. Researchers have observed this "groupthink" tendency in autonomous work groups (Manz and Sims, 1982).

One key reason why GM's early experiment with autonomous groups failed was the absence of periodic reviews to turn up problems and methods of improving the program. INGT's assured anonymity and its avoidance of premature evaluation almost guarantee a productive session when participants are asked: "How can we improve upon the functioning of this program?"

Last, the facilitating effects of INGT provide our best hope for keeping meetings of inexperienced participants, led by inexperienced leaders, from gravitating toward nonproductive bull sessions.

Employees on Boards

The problems of reduced participation due to differences in status and background and to skepticism about fair representation in meetings are greatest in strongly heterogeneous representational groups such as those discussed below.

Codetermination Boards. In a number of countries, laws have been passed that require employee representation on boards of directors. For example, Norway requires that one-third of the director seats be occupied by employee representatives in companies that employ more than fifty people, if the employees so desire. In companies that employ more than two hundred people, employee representation is required (Gustavsen and Humnius, 1981).

Simmons and Mares (1983) report the results of a survey of two hundred Norwegian board members three years after this law went into effect. Eighty percent were fully satisfied. Shareholder-elected members especially liked the improved understanding of company objectives on the part of employees. Employee representatives claimed better insight about company problems and improved influence. Twenty percent had experienced some problem with inadequate secrecy about sensitive information, but did not regard this as a major difficulty.

Cotton and his associates (1985) also found general satisfaction on the part of employee representatives in their survey of some sixty-seven situations in different countries. However, the workers represented were significantly less satisfied, and results relating to effects on performance were quite mixed.

Scanlon, Rucker, and Improshare Plan Committees. Productivity-sharing plans—such as Scanlon, Rucker, and Improshare—have an impressive record of success. Of the thirty successful Scanlon plan companies cited by Moore and Ross (1978), seven permitted the pooling of their financial data. They had paid an average monthly bonus of almost 10 percent above competitive base pay to their employees over a period of ten years.

Mitchell Fein (1982) reports an average 24.4 percent productivity improvement during the first year for fifty-seven companies using his Improshare plan. Workers received 50 percent of the money saved.

The U.S. General Accounting Office (1981) made a study of twenty-four firms representing all three plans. It found that plans in operation more than five years averaged almost 29 percent labor-cost savings for the most recent five-year period. Additional accomplishments commonly cited were better teamwork and cooperation, faster responses to problems, higher product quality, less resistance to change, more employee involvement, and lower rates of absenteeism and turnover.

Management commitment to employee participation in problem identification and problem solving is a key part of all three plans in their most successful form. This commitment must be demonstrated in lower level quality circles (discussed later in this chapter) and in a top level labor-management committee. Mitchell Fein, the originator of Improshare, observes: "In reviewing the plans that do poorly, it becomes clear that management's attitude toward worker involvement has a greater effect on results than any other factor, including the initial attitudes of the employees" (1982, p. 14).

Success also depends upon effective group leadership, not just good intentions. Robert Scott, an authority on the Rucker plan, notes: "A well thought out drive for problem investigation and solution should be introduced at the same time so that the latent brainpower of the employees can be directed toward continuing changes and improvements" (1965, p. 32). And Carl Frost, who worked with Joe Scanlon and founded Scanlon Plan Associates in Lansing, Michigan, observes that "management, whether it is the supervisor in the Production Committee or the executive in the Screening Committee, must exercise genuine leadership in decision making" (1978, p. 31).

Multiple Management. Multiple management, as originated by McCormick and Company of Baltimore, Maryland, provides promising executive, administrative, and professional employees with an opportunity to compete with each other in providing ideas and leadership, while serving on one of several advisory boards set up to develop the means of improving company operations.

At McCormick, there are plant or factory boards, sales boards, and a junior board of directors, each having up to twenty board-elected members, with 20–30 percent of the lowest rated members being replaced every six months on the basis of peer ratings. Members are given extra pay for board service and most inside promotions are made from their ranks. Parliamentary procedure is used and when three-fourths or better voting support is given by a board to a particular proposal, it is referred to the appropriate authority for review.

Multiple management has been highly successful for McCormick. Of 2,109 recommendations made by the first junior board from 1932 through 1936, only six were turned down. And the inputting of good ideas from all of the boards continues, with an estimated acceptance rate, today, of about 80 percent.

McCormick grew from five hundred employees and sales of $4 million in 1932 to 4,669 employees and sales of $251 million in 1975. Seventeen of the company's eighteen senior directors have come up through the junior boards, and some version of multiple management has been adopted by over 500 companies in the United States and abroad (Fox, 1978).

Role of INGT. Survey data from many studies indicate that, in general, employee *codetermination board* members are much more satisfied with the arrangement than are the workers they represent, and the effects on various aspects of lower level performance have been disappointing. This is a serious discrepancy, because our primary concern is with the impact of such representation upon rank-and-file personnel.

Long (1984) reports that employee directors have indicated to him their need for a systematic way to collect inputs on major issues from those they represent. INGT procedures can fill such a need quite effectively. Anonymous inputs can be submitted via conveniently located boxes. Then they can be duplicated and distributed in preparation for INGT meetings at which their relative importance can be determined by constituents. (Chapter

Ten reviews the specific steps for premeeting data collection and the conduct of a problem-identification meeting.)

Substantial differences in status, background, and power commonly exist among the participants of such labor–management boards, and these differences detract from productive group performance, particularly during the first months of attempted collaboration. As Mitchell Fein, originator of Improshare, observes: "Changing from traditional to consultative practices is a giant step for most employees, who are usually timid in the presence of management members. Even strong union committee members are sometimes overawed by managers" (Fein, 1981, p. 60). The anonymous inputting and display features of INGT deal effectively with this problem.

The general success of productivity-sharing committees in the United States is well established; however, there is reason to believe that these groups could function even better, were they to use the Improved Nominal Group Technique, at least periodically. There are several potentially beneficial features. For example, INGT's permanent display record (on flipchart pages) will be of value for two reasons.

First, such groups often must adjourn with unfinished business, sometimes for several weeks. The permanent display record permits the group to pick up where it left off, without wasteful backtracking or the loss of good ideas.

Second, the display materials provide an effective means for briefing constituents and others who did not attend the meetings. Key elements of the group's decision-making process can be recreated from beginning to end: the total array of ideas considered, deletions and changes which were made, and the allocation of votes. These things become a matter of record, rather than the imperfect product of conjecture or selective recall. Additionally, these materials assure that a group will get full credit for the quality of its efforts.

When employees and management vote to adopt a Scanlon-like plan, they get a prescribed set of new procedures and committees. James Driscoll (1985) points out that these proven structures help to build commitment through time. Periodic reviews of the new structures via INGT meetings devoted to the question: "How can we improve upon this system?" should further enhance both commitment and organizational functioning.

Driscoll also indicates that a "peaking-out" of interest and involvement often occurs after obvious problems and opportunities for increasing productivity have been covered. He suggests that the best antidote at that point is to "feed the plan": to submit larger problems to the labor–management committees. INGT procedures will aid committees greatly in dealing with increased problem complexity; the procedures for collecting and reviewing premeeting inputs (see Chapter Four) and for reviewing proposed solutions (see Chapter Eight) should prove especially useful.

Many labor–management committees become quite large in order to properly represent their constituencies. This creates information overload and disorderly process. A common reaction is to formalize problem solving and document review activity through the adoption of parliamentary procedure. Unfortunately, this so-called solution usually penalizes collaborative effort. Based on a study of many groups, Guetzkow and Gyr (1954) found that in most cases parliamentary procedure did *not* facilitate movement toward genuine consensus.

The INGT guidelines for conducting a meeting provide a constructive alternative. They permit us to maintain the participative opportunities and climate of a small group efficiently and effectively with up to twenty participants. And if we wish to assign the same purpose to several groups simultaneously, Chapter Nine presents an effective means for melding and building upon the voting results obtained.

A multiple management board will not want to utilize the leadership guidelines and anonymous inputting of INGT when it is primarily concerned with assessing the initiative, leadership skills, and thinking of individual members. Probably, these purposes are best served by the maintenance of a competitive arena.

However, when the assessment process is largely complete, a shift to INGT will provide for more effective group problem identification and problem solving, and it will acquaint participants with the best procedures for encouraging and sustaining constructive involvement on the part of the groups they lead or will lead.

Senior boards of directors and others who review written recommendations from various multiple management boards or other groups will find the INGT document review procedure to be a time-saving and efficient approach.

Finally we address the question: "Why spend meeting time on things we can do as well or better on our own?" Most of the participants who serve on the types of boards we've discussed in this section are quite busy. They can benefit greatly from the use of premeeting participation (see Chapter Four). It produces a beachhead of ideas which all can build upon. It permits adjustments in decisions about reference materials or resource people to involve in the meeting. And, it permits all who will attend to prepare themselves in advance so they can get the most benefit from interacting with each other.

Quality Circles

Typically, quality circles are formed to identify and solve work-related problems (other than those which deal with employee complaints, pay policies, personalities, and hiring and firing policies). Quality circles comprise three to twelve volunteers who meet with their supervisor once a week on company time; although, occasionally, a group will prefer to appoint a fellow worker as leader, with the supervisor serving as a member of the group or as an aide to it.

Usually, groups are trained in data collection methods (such as sampling techniques and the use of check drawings, check lists, control charts, histograms, and other types of graphs) and in methods of analyzing data (such as Pareto analysis and the use of cause and effect diagrams), as well as in group dynamics. Sometimes, more advanced analytical techniques such as sensitivity analysis are included in training (Ingle, 1982).

In 1974 in the United States Donnelly Mirrors of Holland, Michigan, enriched its successful Scanlon plan with the formation of some seventy quality circles (Hill, 1974). By 1982, over 2,500 firms had active quality circles according to a responsible estimate

(Mento, 1982). Over 100,000 circles had been registered in Japan a year earlier, with an additional 1,000,000 unregistered circles estimated (Ouchi, 1981).

These figures suggest that it is easy to start and sustain successful quality circles, but this is not so. Cole (1980) reports that only one-third of the Japanese circles are working well, even in plants which are noted for the best quality circle programs. Research here shows that only about one-fourth of the initially successful U.S. programs survive more than a few years (Goodman, 1980).

Among the chief reasons for failure are poor group process and leadership. The coordinator of a successful program at Mercury Marine, located in Fond du Lac, Wisconsin, points to several of the problems associated with conventional procedures: one or two individuals dominating the discussion, others holding back their ideas, and those who constantly argue for the sake of arguing (Ingle, 1982). The importance of group leadership is also stressed in studies by Imberman (1982), Seelye and Sween (1983), and White and Bednar (1983).

In reviewing reasons for the failure of quality circles, another investigator reports: "Teams would sometimes spend too much time deciding *how* they were going to approach an issue rather than spending the time actually discussing the issue." However, when each group was given a trained, outside facilitator to keep group process moving, and the goal of coming up with the five most important problems facing the group, participants concentrated on the task at hand and stopped worrying about process issues. One member commented to the investigator that "these task teams accomplished more in the first two hours than my quality circle did in three months" (Kushell, 1985).

Ingle observes: "Some members miss meetings, some keep interrupting the meetings by introducing unrelated topics. Here again the facilitator is the one who should watch for such a condition, find out the reasons, and then apply positive thinking and actions to modify the moods of the meetings" (1982, p. 55).

Quality circles must be free to focus their energies on identifying and solving problems. They need to get the most out of each session, and they need to make proposals to higher management as efficiently as possible, because at all levels the time available for meetings is costly and scarce. Also, quality circles should avoid unnecessary duplication of effort by reviewing the deliberations and proposed solutions of other circles working on similar or related problems.

The Improved Nominal Group Technique provides facilitators with the ideal means for satisfying these requirements. After helping group leaders master the procedures described in this book, facilitators need only periodically check to see if the procedures are being followed. Facilitators will then have more time to support their groups by (1) helping them obtain needed technical information; (2) lining up special resource people whose attendance at a meeting is suggested by premeeting inputs; and (3) locating other circles who are working on similar problems. In addition, the positive effects of INGT training will provide facilitators with more opportunities to give deserved praise to group leaders for a job well done.

The Improved Nominal Group Technique produces optimal participant contribution through the anonymous inputting of ideas before and during a meeting, the complete display and deferred evaluation of these inputs, a significant reduction in interpersonal conflict and domination attempts (on the part of leaders as well as others), and the minimization of wasted time.

The anonymous voting procedures get us as close as we can get to the true sentiments of participants, and the permanent record of all inputs and changes facilitates the utilization of special resource people by the group and review of the group's deliberations at a later date.

Finally, the document review meeting procedures provide those who must evaluate and approve written proposals with the most efficient means, and the procedures for INGT multiple-group functioning show how we can effectively integrate the simultaneous deliberations of several groups working on the same assignment.

For the long haul as well as the present, the unequaled participation power of INGT provides the best hope for keeping quality circles from going stale after an initial burst of enthusiasm. From time to time, this unique power should be focused on the topic: "How can we improve upon the operation of our quality circle?"

Survey Feedback

Attitude survey programs can provide valuable data for monitoring the health of an organization and for prompting needed problem solving and corrective action, but such programs will backfire if all they produce is talk and neatly filed reports. Few of us want to identify deficiencies in leadership and other work-related problems "for fun"; rather, we tend to become cynical when we are left empty-handed after having had our hopes for needed change encouraged.

Ultimately we must depend on immediate supervisors for a successful *survey feedback program,* since most of the corrective action that will be needed will fall within the domain of their groups. Unfortunately, those leaders associated with the poorest survey results, and therefore with the greatest opportunities for improvement, are usually the ones who will be most reluctant and least prepared to respond constructively.

Characteristically, they failed to create conditions for effective problem identification and problem solving in the past and will be less inclined to start doing so in the face of perceived rejection. They feel particularly threatened by the prospect of any kind of truly collaborative meeting with their subordinates, because they feel that those who rated them poorly will have the upper hand and will undoubtedly use it to give them a hard time.

Under these conditions, forcing unprepared supervisors to attempt collaborative problem solving can be disastrous. It is much more productive to prepare them through sound *behavior modeling* training, such as that which IBM's five-module Survey Feedback Techniques program employs (Dodd and Pesci, 1977). Through rehearsal of appropriate learning points, supervisors master useful procedures for presenting and processing survey data, as they develop confidence in their ability to maintain control in a positive manner.

The addition of INGT procedures should enhance a group's ability to diagnose the data and develop useful proposals. In particular, the anonymous inputting and display features will make it easier for sensitive issues, such as problems created by the supervisor's behavior, to surface and be dealt with in a less personal and less threatening manner. And, the clear-cut, facilitative character of the discussion guidelines will further strengthen the supervisor's confidence in his or her ability to maintain control in a positive manner.

Chapter Thirteen

Bargaining, Project, and Venture Teams and Other Ad Hoc Groups

Chapter Twelve discussed the uses of the Improved Nominal Group Technique (INGT) for relatively permanent groups. This chapter presents INGT's special advantages for various types of temporary groups, such as *bargaining teams, confrontation meeting committees, project teams, and venture teams.*

Usually, temporary groups have a limited amount of time to finish their work. The sooner they can set priorities and start to solve problems, the better. Yet, fast start-ups are difficult for them since group members usually come from different work units and are not accustomed to working with each other. They need time for the "feeling-out" process that new conventional groups normally require to develop successful working relationships.

INGT permits groups to get "up to speed" faster, because it emphasizes the quality of an idea rather than authorship, prevents premature evaluation of ideas, and discourages infighting among group members. Other special advantages that INGT can afford various types of ad hoc groups are discussed below.

Bargaining Teams

Harvard University's Negotiation Project has developed a promising approach called *Principled Negotiation* (Fisher and

Ury, 1983), a process that helps either party of a bargaining relationship move toward a fair agreement. Although it should be equally effective for individual and group use, we are concerned here with its use by a bargaining team.

Those aspects of Principled Negotiation which can draw on the unique advantages of the Improved Nominal Group Technique are

1. *Determine our interests.* What are our needs, desires, and fears with regard to outcomes from the negotiation? And in what order of importance?

2. *What are their interests?* If we do not know, and the other side won't tell us, let's do our best to determine their interests and their relative importance by putting our heads together. (We will need to have this information to satisfy the following item.)

3. *What are the best options for mutual gain?* If we want only the peeling to make marmalade, and the other side wants only the orange to eat, we can both have the "whole orange." By discovering such options, we can increase the size of the pie to be divided to our mutual benefit. Fisher and Ury (1983) observe that most people do not associate such creative problem solving with the negotiation process, but it can pay handsome dividends when they do. They suggest the possibility of inviting the other side to participate in a group session devoted to discovering mutual gain options.

4. *What standard, or source, of arbitration should we use?* If we reach an impasse on one or more issues, and the standard, or source, of arbitration for resolving the matter is not obvious, we should develop and evaluate a list of possibilities.

5. *What is our best alternative to a negotiated agreement?* If the other side out guns us and insists on "hanging tough," what is our bottom line for entering into an agreement? Obviously, the most we will be willing to give depends upon the utility of the best alternative to a negotiated settlement available to us. If this alternative is not apparent, we should use our collective effort to identify it.

6. *What is their best alternative?* Perhaps the other side is bluffing about its bottom line? Perhaps it is too optimistic about the availability of good alternatives to a settlement with us. If our

problem-solving efforts indicate this to be likely, we have a good basis for improving our bottom line position (Fisher and Ury, 1983).

All of the activities listed above involve the identification and evaluation of positions and options. The premeeting and meeting procedures of INGT are ideally suited to these purposes. Additionally, INGT's ability to minimize interpersonal conflict and attempts to dominate make it particularly valuable when opposing parties search for mutual gain options in a joint meeting.

Fisher and Ury imply their support of INGT by listing the following guidelines for identifying and evaluating options:

- Appoint someone to keep the meeting on track.
- Separate the process of originating options from that of selecting from among them.
- Record the ideas in full view of all participants.
- Make sure that everyone gets a chance to speak.
- Avoid premature judgment.
- Avoid premature closure.

As we have seen, INGT goes far beyond merely listing these important objectives. It shows specifically how to accomplish them. In addition, it provides for anonymous inputting, productive premeeting activity, and authentic voting.

Confrontation Meeting Committees

A confrontation meeting involves having personnel, drawn from all levels of an organization, take a quick reading on the organization's health, usually within a period of four to five hours. Participants are assigned to small heterogeneous groups, ensuring that no bosses are placed together with their own subordinates. Each group is instructed to identify problems that confront the organization, and to report back to the larger group. Next, problems are assigned to appropriate work units or special teams for resolution.

This intensive, organization-wide approach has been used successfully on many occasions. Beckhard indicates that this approach is particularly appropriate when there is some urgency for such a review. The need can arise from an unexpected crisis or the fact that the organization has recently undergone a major change (Beckhard, 1967; Beckhard and Harris, 1977).

The Improved Nominal Group Technique is ideally suited to the problem-identification and problem-solving activities of various confrontation meeting groups. And the document review meeting provides an unusually effective means for higher management to review and evaluate the written proposals of these groups.

Project Teams

A project team comprised of appropriate personnel from different parts of an organization is formed to carry out some assigned mission. The mission might be to plan and implement a merger or reorganization, to develop a new product, or to perform some other one-time undertaking. Larger teams often form subteams to work on different facets of their project, and both will likely want to draw upon the expertise of internal or external consultants from time to time.

In addition to the advantages that INGT affords any group engaged in identifying and evaluating problems, positions, options, and solutions, INGT affords project teams special protection against several problems which affect them in particular.

One of these is a problem of discontinuity of effort and contact. Some participants serve on several projects simultaneously in addition to retaining ongoing obligations to their regular functional supervisors. It is natural for them to favor a project that best matches their interests, but this can cause them to be absent or tardy with regard to other project team meetings. This lack of continuity can seriously interfere with their ability to contribute.

The permanent display materials developed by INGT minimize these discontinuity problems. They permit anyone to easily recreate the key elements of a team's process from start to finish.

Also, the display materials make it possible for teams to receive full credit for the quality of their efforts. Projects run into unexpected problems and undeserved failures. It is important for team morale and fair appraisal, in those instances, that there exists an effective basis for monitoring what was considered, and with what degree of thoroughness.

Leading project teams effectively can be difficult. In addition to the discontinuity problems mentioned above, assigned leaders are often younger and less experienced than some of their team members, and they usually have little if any control over the final performance appraisals and other material rewards that members receive. They may not have worked with many of the participants before, yet, they are expected to get the team "up and running" fast, with little time for a "feeling-out" process. INGT's explicit procedures compensate for a leader's lack of familiarity with a group as well as any lack of experience with group leadership.

Finally, the document review meeting provides an excellent means for the project team to review the written proposals of its subteams, as well as for higher management to review the written proposals of the project team.

Volunteer Venture Teams

Based upon their survey of many companies, Peters and Waterman (1982) report the impressive track record for innovation achieved by volunteer venture teams led by volunteer "champions," working on their own ideas in organizations that nurture their efforts and reward their successes handsomely.

A clear majority of groups led by champions succeed; whereas, an overwhelming majority of groups without such leadership fail. It is interesting to note that this same phenomenon is observed in Japan. An IBM manager concludes: "It's just amazing what a handful of dedicated people can do when they are really turned on" (Peters and Waterman, 1982, p. 205).

But the same fanatic determination and egoism which characterize champions pose a barrier to getting the best creative problem-solving efforts from a group. Arrogance and impatience do not create a favorable collaborative climate, even for volunteers. Champions can safeguard their groups against this danger, in addition to gaining the other benefits we have discussed, by committing themselves to the use of the Improved Nominal Group Technique.

Diagnosis for Job Redesign

Sometimes, low employee motivation and low job satisfaction are due to a mismatch between the kind of people we have and want to keep and the restricted stimulation and limited opportunities provided by their jobs. True, some jobs are the way they are unavoidably, due to constraints imposed by technology, labor contracts, or other factors. However, traditional job structures are often maintained for no reason other than inertia or inattention.

Miner's (1980) review of research studies shows what appropriate job redesign can accomplish in enhanced employee satisfaction and performance. Hackman and Oldham (1980), authors of the current job characteristics theory of work redesign, provide criteria for deciding when redesign is feasible and guidelines for accomplishing such redesign.

Sound diagnosis is the key to making a good decision about whether or not to redesign a particular job. We need to determine the extent to which problems are being created by the job, itself, or by other factors in the job environment. To do this properly, we need to use several methods for collecting information. Hackman and Oldham (1980, Appendixes A–E) present two, field-tested instruments for this purpose: the *Job Diagnostic Survey* for present job incumbents and the *Job Rating Form* for nonincumbents.

We can check on the data we obtain with these instruments and get important additional information by using the Improved Nominal Group Technique. An appropriate question for job incumbents would be "What things keep you from doing a better job and from being more satisfied with your job?"

Chapter Fourteen

Organization Development and Quality-of-Work-Life Programs

One characteristic that distinguishes organization development (OD) from other approaches for improving organizational effectiveness is an emphasis on collaborative diagnosis, problem solving, and action (French and Bell, 1984). In fact, when one of the special programs discussed in the preceding chapters incorporates this collaborative emphasis, we often find it involved in an organization development program.

A key function of the OD consultant or facilitator, then, is to support the establishment and maintenance of a collaborative action–research process that contributes to the development of individual and group capabilities for coping with problems for the future as well as the present. The more informed choices that participants can (and will) identify and evaluate, the better.

Consequently, the very essence of organization development imposes the following conclusion: A basic requirement for OD success is an organizational commitment to reject any condition that would discourage or block effective collaboration in the present or future. And no approach can better serve this commitment than the one presented in this book, the Improved Nominal Group Technique, for the reasons which follow.

Opportunity to Participate Is the Key

At any given time, some group members will not want to participate. They should not be required to, but it should be clear to them that the opportunity will always be present. This approach is consistent with one of the most important findings we have about the employee–job relationship: the more control a worker perceives he or she has over the work situation, the better she or he will withstand the physical and psychological pressures that occur (Frankenhauser and Gardell, 1976). In this context, control means opportunity for an active relationship with problems, not necessarily active involvement.

This distinction is illustrated by a study in which subjects who engaged in proofreading and in trying to solve insoluble puzzles were exposed to unpleasant, randomly occurring noise. Half of the subjects had access to a noise cut-off button with instructions to use it if the noise became too much for them; the other half had no escape option.

As it turned out, those with the button attempted almost five times as many puzzles and made significantly fewer omissions in proofreading than the other group, despite the fact that they never used it! Their awareness that they could use it was the controlling difference (Glass, Singer, and Friedman, 1969).

Other studies show that low-demand work can have negative effects upon workers as can high-demand work. Karasek's (1981) findings accommodate both of these situations within the context of perceived control. We can better visualize his findings using Table 4. We see that the two most favorable conditions are associated with high perceived control over job-related decisions, and that low dissatisfaction continues to be associated with high perceived control when output pressure becomes high.

In a study of 250 teachers in seventeen elementary schools, Mohrman (1979) found that perceived opportunity to influence decisions was strongly related to measures of trust and organizational effectiveness, but the actual amount of participation was not. In a study of sixty experienced sewing machine operators, Fleishman (1965) found that direct participation by everyone in

Table 4. The Effects of Perceived Control.

Perceived Control over Job-Related Decisions	Output Pressure	
	Low	*High*
Low	Moderate Mental Strain High Dissatisfaction	High Mental Strain Higher Dissatisfaction
High	Low Mental Strain Low Dissatisfaction	Moderate Mental Strain Low Dissatisfaction

Note: Mental Strain: Anxiety, nervousness, sleeping and relaxation problems, difficulty in getting started in the morning (data from 1,016 U.S. workers provide the same pattern as data from 1,896 Swedish workers).

Job Dissatisfaction: Job-related depression symptoms and willingness to leave job (based upon U.S. sample; no Swedish data available).

production planning for a work style change was not as critical a factor as the group's perception of effective representation in the matter.

Supervisors share this need for influence potential. In a study of twelve geographically dispersed plants of a manufacturing firm, McMahon (1976) found that the satisfaction of first-level managers and their positive perceptions of various aspects of organizational functioning were strongly associated with the amount of influence they were perceived to have.

The importance of perceived control is supported, also, by research findings associated with *Tannenbaum's Control Theory.* Organization members are asked to indicate on a five-point scale how much control, defined as the capacity to manipulate available means for the satisfaction of needs, they perceive that individuals at each organization level exert. Key findings (Miner, 1982) are

• There is *not* a fixed amount of total control within an organization. It can go up or down; therefore, participative management does not necessarily reduce the influence of managers.

- Organizations that have *both* influential managers and influential subordinates tend to be more effective than those with less influential managers and/or subordinates. The total amount of control is positively associated with organizational effectiveness in a wide range of situations.
- Participative approaches are associated with greater amounts of total control, and coercive supervisory practices are associated with smaller amounts of total control.

Remaining on the Sidelines. Some people choose to participate far less than others, even after extended exposure to genuine participation opportunities in the work setting. For example, in one long-term study, the following question was posed to employees after they had been associated with autonomous work teams: "If you had a choice of otherwise identical jobs, would the prospect of participating in decisions be important enough to lead you to choosing the participatory job?" Only 50 percent said yes (Witte, 1980, p. 150). Although it is likely that a larger proportion would respond positively in other situations, the company in this particular example was faced with special problems; it seems improbable that a positive response rate would approach 100 percent.

Even those who do participate frequently are inclined to show some selectivity in doing so. For example, in describing such workers from the study mentioned above, Witte reports that "although they clearly expressed the strongest desire to participate in areas that most directly affected their work . . . support for participation was much less in those critical areas that suggested the possibility of interpersonal conflict and the application of sanctions by the group" (1980, p. 132).

These findings suggest that we cannot determine whether or not participation is "just right," without comparing *actual* participation in areas of interest to the participant with *desired* participation in those areas, on an individual by individual basis.

Further support for this view is provided by the results of a study of 154 project engineers by Ivancevich (1979). Many individuals who felt they were underparticipating actually participated in more decisions than many who felt they were overparticipating, and the number of participation areas desired by those individuals who felt their level of participation was just right ranged from one to eight. Of equal interest, overparticipation appeared to pose as great a problem as did underparticipation.

It is difficult to tell who will want to contribute when and on what issues. And, individual differences vary about different socially acceptable levels of involvement, depending upon the particular culture or subculture represented. In any particular group, these norms can change, but the process takes time. The important thing for individual leaders to do, with aid from their organizations, is to maintain the opportunity—to sustain the perception of control potential.

Role of INGT. The Improved Nominal Group Technique (INGT) optimizes perceived participation opportunity, while minimizing the possibilities for intimidation and forced participation, through the following features:

- Anonymous premeeting inputting of ideas;
- Anonymous in-meeting inputting of ideas;
- The ability of an individual to block the revision or removal of an item on display without explanation;
- Assurance that no adoptive group action will be taken on any given item until discussion opportunity has been provided for all items;
- Anonymous voting; and
- The clear responsibility given the group leader to protect every group member from forced involvement (such as having to defend a position).

The Two Faces of Power

The exercise of power—the capacity to bring about desired outcomes—is essential to the effective operation of any group or organization. It is also a key determinant of the fortunes of an organization development (OD) program. The critical issue is how it is used.

In this regard, McClelland (1970) provides us with a useful distinction between its positive and negative faces. The leader who uses power positively benefits both himself and his group members: shared objectives are pursued with mutual trust and respect, and the leader makes no attempt to benefit personally at their expense. Clearly, this is the power orientation which is suited to OD's collaborative, action–research process.

The negative use of power is just the opposite: the need to dominate submissive individuals, solely for the benefit of the dominator. Whether or not the dominated benefit or lose in the process is of little concern.

When the negative power leader is faced with top management commitment to an OD effort, she or he will typically respond by paying lip service to the idea of participation while continuing to dominate and manipulate subordinate group process. Without some type of appropriate structuring of what goes on below, it is very difficult for top management to prevent this type of duplicity.

INGT provides the control. It is a welcome tool to the positive power leader, because it is so facilitative of the collaborative, action–research process. At the same time, it stands a good chance of blocking the subversive attempts of the negative power leader. Its requirements are so explicit and straightforward, one cannot easily pay lip service to them and then abandon or prostitute them in practice.

To improve an OD program's chances for success, have all leaders agree to try INGT with their groups for the initial identification and prioritizing of problems and/or solving a particular problem. Then, have leaders poll members anonymously to see if they want to retain INGT, or any part of it, in place of their customary procedures. This approach is inherently more appealing than what Rosabeth Kanter terms "the irony of participation by command" or the situations she has observed where "participation is something the top orders the middle to do for the bottom" (1983, pp. 244, 245).

Management of Change

By definition, organization development is concerned with change, and change in one part of an organization can impact on operations and people in other parts. When large change efforts are not managed properly, we invite the emergence of resisting behaviors, which undermine morale and increase costs. In some cases, such resistance can block change altogether.

Many believe that resistance to change is just part of human nature. But think about it. Would you resist an unexpected raise in pay? Or the surprise approval of an assignment to highly desired work? Of course not; we resist only those changes that we perceive have a net effect of threatening or inconveniencing us.

When we are not sure or have no idea what effect changes in the work environment will have upon us, we are likely to feel threatened. Negative reactions include passing on disquieting rumors, talking against management and the changes, and even looking for another job. Tragically, many who would benefit from changes, but are not clearly aware of this, respond the same way as those who would not benefit.

The appointment of a team for the management of change, comprised of representatives of affected units and headed by a knowledgeable insider of high status, can do much to minimize such problems. The team can solicit perceptions about the impact of the proposed changes before they are made and make recommendations for more effective implementation and explanation. By doing this regularly, the team can stay in touch with, and in control of, the inevitable technical bugs and human resistances which accompany any major change effort.

A key determinant of the team's success is its ability to accurately monitor these problems, resentments, and fears as they develop. An outside consultant can help with this. INGT provides even greater help. Its anonymous premeeting and in-meeting inputting features encourage distrustful people to "tell it like it is," and the display and direction of discussion features provide sound means for constructively resolving the sensitive issues that surface.

New Design or "Greenfield" Plants

One of the most fruitful expressions of organization development in practice is the new design or greenfield plant. It is a fresh-start undertaking, based upon current sociotechnical systems design concepts, to provide concurrent optimization of productivity, quality of work life, and organizational adaptability.

A well-publicized example is Saturn Corporation, General Motors' new automotive subsidiary. Its goal of making small cars that are cost competitive with any imports is to be achieved by blending technology on the cutting edge with a team approach to production and a high degree of employee participation in decision making.

Not as well known are the new design or greenfield projects of other companies. Lawler (1986) reports that AT&T, General Foods, PPG Industries, Procter & Gamble, Sherwin-Williams, TRW, H. J. Heinz, Rockwell, Johnson & Johnson, General Motors, Mead, Cummins Engine, and some twenty-eight other firms are estimated to be responsible for about two hundred such undertakings.

When we consider that Procter & Gamble has built over twenty of these; has mandated that *all* of its new plants will be of this high-employee involvement type; and, more recently, has ordered *all* of its traditional plants to convert to this approach, it seems reasonable to conclude that the program has been highly successful.

Most of the decision making in these new plants is done in work teams and in interunit task forces, involving many types of problems and opportunities. As Lawler points out, first-level supervisors and elected group leaders urgently need effective means for getting the most from group process without wasting valuable group time. In addition, they are sometimes at a loss as to what to do about the handling of issues for which they already have all of the information and technical expertise needed.

Although new design plant personnel may not face some of the problems associated with moving existing work groups toward more meaningful participation, they will still face others: lower status individuals withholding their thinking for fear of appearing foolish to better-educated participants, the time-consuming "feeling-out" process often required for new interunit task forces to get up to speed, tendencies toward "groupthink" in highly committed groups, and the ever-present challenge to control nonproductive individual behavior without undermining a positive climate for problem solving.

INGT procedures eliminate or minimize these problems for the reasons we have discussed. In addition, because of their makeup and temporary nature, interunit task forces can make particularly good use of the display sheets for briefing those who are late or miss a meeting, as well as any nonparticipants who are affected. The display sheets are also useful for communicating the breadth and quality of inputs processed to managers elsewhere who may be skeptical about the ability of rank-and-file teams to engage in meaningful problem-solving activity.

The document review meeting provides an excellent answer to the question: "What should a participative leader do about handling an issue for which she or he already has all of the information and technical expertise needed?" There is no need for game playing; she or he can simply submit the information in the form of a detailed proposal to a document review meeting with the charge: "How can we improve upon this?" Some useful refinements are likely to emerge. At the very least, the process will likely produce greater understanding and acceptance on the part of the participants than unilateral prescription could produce, while maintaining a participative climate.

OD in the Sunshine

All states have "government in the sunshine" laws which require public employees to assure public access to most of their group deliberations and to use nonsecret voting in making decisions. These laws protect the public against collusion; however, they seriously discourage many public employees from identifying and solving problems in a straightforward manner, for most public employees are inherently more vulnerable than other people to the constraining factors discussed in this chapter and in Chapter Two.

Golembiewski (1985), an OD consultant with broad experience in the public sector, draws upon this experience and that of others to explain the source of this heightened vulnerability. For public employees, the pursuit of personal advantage and security assumes greater importance in the presence of the unstable and often conflicting agency goals that result from the demands of competing constituencies. This is especially true in the absence of "hard" outcome measures coupled with the discipline of a profit and loss statement.

Survival in the uncertain political milieu is aided by equivocation. It minimizes the making of enemies and it helps one to end up on the "winning side," which usually beats losing, even when later events prove that one was right. Public officials are attractive targets to hostile special interest groups and to uninformed individuals who take simple stands and seek quick fixes for complex problems and issues. Public officials are particularly sensitive to the possibility of being quoted out of context by reporters in search of attention-grabbing stories.

These conditions give added advantage to the use of anonymity for problem identification and problem solving. Presumably, all of the procedures we've advocated, with the exception of secret voting, are compatible with various "sunshine laws." Even the anonymous first vote (see pages 61–65) may be legal in some states.

In any event, the provisions for anonymous inputting, both before and during a meeting, coupled with INGT's discussion guidelines, should improve the productivity of public meetings for the purposes of OD and other problem-solving activities. Anonymous inputting increases productivity by encouraging useful inputs and discouraging various forms of political gamesmanship.

Role of the Facilitator

One of the key objectives to the OD facilitator is to encourage and guide the establishment and maintenance of a collaborative action–research process that will nurture the development of individual and group problem-solving abilities. In this regard, it is interesting that Manz and Sims (1984) found that emergent leaders of self-managing groups, as well as members of top management, identified "facilitation of problem-solving process" as a top priority function for coordinators (or facilitators).

In preceding sections, we have seen how INGT:

- Identifies objectives that are most congruent with organizational and personal needs;
- Provides for a frank review of rules, policies, procedures, proposals, and programs without wasting time;
- Discourages "groupthink" in highly cohesive groups;
- Sets the stage for more fruitful meetings through the collection and distribution of premeeting inputs;
- Encourages the process of bringing sensitive issues to the surface to be dealt with in a less-personal and less-threatening way;
- Minimizes personal dominance and "shooting the bull";
- Generates display materials that minimize problems of discontinuity of effort and contact by permitting comprehensive self-briefing and the briefing of others about group process and outcomes;
- Reduces the "feeling-out" process normally required for new groups to get down to business;
- Provides a useful resource for checking on the candor of diagnostic data about job redesign obtained with other instruments;
- Permits expert authorities to input useful data without chilling the climate for participation; and
- Supports the perception of the opportunity for influence, despite one's current level of involvement, while encouraging additional involvement.

Thus, INGT procedures provide the OD facilitator with concrete, operational means for achieving important OD goals. By mastering them, training groups in their use, and subsequently having only to monitor this usage, the facilitator will have more time to assist groups in the following ways:

- Helping them obtain needed technical information;
- Lining up special resource people whose attendance is suggested by premeeting inputs or by the filed display materials from past group meetings;
- Locating other groups that are working on similar problems to permit the cross-fertilization of ideas; and
- Troubleshooting and helping management to evaluate the overall program.

Additionally, commitment to the use of INGT procedures on the part of leaders and their groups sets the stage for OD facilitators to monitor opportunities for organization-wide involvement over time, accurately, nonobtrusively, and with nominal effort. The explicit procedures are hard to subvert on the sly, and the display materials tell much about what actually did or did not occur.

Maintaining the Gains

After reviewing the experience of a number of initially successful *quality-of-work-life* (QWL) improvement programs, Nightingale (1984) concludes that the difference between continuing success and almost assured failure is a commitment to making periodic assessments to determine if changing needs and expectations are being met. He asserts: "No matter how strong the initial spirit of goodwill when the program is conceived and implemented, the program should not be considered as the final point. . . . Unfortunately, however, a powerful patron too often becomes enamoured of his or her original concept and is often unwilling to subject it to continuing review and appraisal" (pp. 461, 472).

Nightingale illustrates the need for continuing review through a case study of a firm that employed 350 people in three locations. Its highly successful QWL program almost failed on several occasions, despite the positive climate created by the firm's employee ownership and profit-sharing programs. Complacency generated by success was the underlying problem each time.

INGT's anonymous premeeting and in-meeting inputting procedures provide the best means for monitoring the health of a program. Even when we are confident that everything is fine, we should periodically challenge INGT-led groups with the question: "How can we improve upon the functioning of this program?"

In Conclusion

The purpose of the Improved Nominal Group Technique is to aid groups, not hinder them. It is adaptive to changing needs and circumstances. It can be used in whole or in part.

Groups, as well as individuals, can grow in maturity and commitment. At an appropriate time, a group may find it useful to experiment with relaxing some of INGT's constraints. For example, under the right conditions, strenuous debate can be both stimulating and productive. In this regard, a study by Schweiger, Sandberg, and Ragan (1986) indicates that the *Dialectical Inquiry* approach shows promise. It involves in-depth debating of two different recommendations based upon contrary assumptions but developed from the same data (Mason and Mitroff, 1981).

In time, group members may feel less need for the anonymity provided by repeated card collection rounds and resort more to verbal inputting after the first round of anonymous inputting.

But do not abandon any part of INGT before you try it, because each part is based upon solid research and experience. And if departure from a given rule or procedure proves to be premature or counterproductive, quickly reinstate that rule or procedure through group action.

Chapter Fifteen

Audio, Video, and Computer Teleconferencing

Interdependent decision makers find life more complicated when they are physically dispersed to different locations. Repeatedly, they find themselves checking back with colleagues and worrying about decision deadlines when they are forced to rely upon one-on-one telephone conversations in place of interactive meetings.

On the other hand, traveling for the purpose of getting together has its drawbacks. Long-distance trips interfere with natural eating and sleeping cycles, remove us from many productive activities within and outside of our work groups, and can be quite expensive. Even the organization of a crosstown meeting can be time-consuming and disruptive.

These disadvantages, coupled with the demonstrated values of participative problem solving, have directed increasing attention in recent years to various forms of teleconferencing as a means of getting people together. The extent of this interest is indicated by the estimate of 4.2 to 4.5 million teleconferences in 1986 made by Elliot Gold, publisher of the *TeleSpan Newsletter* (private conversation with author).

We can define teleconferencing as any system that provides for interactive communication among three or more people, in two or more locations, through electronic means. Basically, there are four forms: audio-only conferencing, audio conferencing

141

with graphics transmission, video conferencing, and computer conferencing. We will now consider key characteristics of these forms, how users react to them, and how Improved Nominal Group Technique (INGT) can enhance their effectiveness.

Audio-Only Conferencing

One person with access to a TouchTone telephone with an asterisk button can organize a teleconference easily and inexpensively. The procedure is simple. The leader calls a group member, instructs him or her not to hang up, puts that line on hold by pushing the asterisk button; calls another group member, puts that line on hold; and so on. After acquiring the last teleconferee, the leader pushes the asterisk button a second time to enter the network.

This can work fine, provided there is just one person at each telephone site, the number of participants is small, the total system is working well with sufficient volume, and there is no need to transmit graphics during the conference. However, if any of these conditions must be met or if you would like additional participants to be able to join an ongoing conference (or to rejoin it if accidently disconnected), you need to explore the pros and cons of special equipment, accommodations, and services. According to Robert Cowan (1984), a good way to start is to buy a copy of *TeleSpan's Definitive Guide to Teleconferencing Products and Services* (published by TeleSpan Publishing Corp., Altadena, Calif.).

In addition to addressing special needs, service companies. like ConferTech, Connex, Darome, Kellogg Communications, and Tele/Link, use a "meet me" approach which eliminates the need to enter a holding mode until all conferees are on the network. This system works for up to two hundred participants, here and abroad. Each is given an access code to dial so that all can "meet" on an electronic conference "bridge" at the same time (Kelleher and Cross, 1985). Some companies also provide information hotlines and teleconference workshops.

Audio Conferencing with Graphics Transmission

In addition to the features of audio-only conferencing, this mode adds fast graphics transmission capability. It can be provided by several means, including: Group 3 or 4 facsimile (FAX) machines; Telewriters; a computer network; The Discon Writing Surface; The Electronic Blackboard; The Excom; Slow-Scan (SSTV), or "freeze-frame," television; Wang's PIC; and remote-control, random-access microfiche and slide projectors. There is little question that it pays to make a careful assessment of the pros and cons of each alternative. In addition to TeleSpan's guide mentioned earlier, there is a useful book for this purpose by Kelleher and Cross entitled *Teleconferencing: Linking People Together Electronically* (Prentice-Hall, 1985).

The *TeleSpan Newsletter* (1983) reported that the East Lansing Research Association in Michigan estimated that 90 percent of all teleconferences held in 1983–84 were primarily audio teleconferences. They further estimated that this percentage would drop to 80 percent of all teleconferences held in 1986–87. Part of this usage is accounted for by Honeywell's successful program.

In the late 1970s, dedicated, AT&T-planned teleconference rooms, with multiple graphics capabilities, were constructed at six major Honeywell facilities to link with nondedicated facilities at other lower-utilization sites. After two years, growing utilization resulted in the addition of eight more dedicated rooms. Now, locations in Mexico and Europe use portable teleconferencing equipment for regular meetings with Honeywell's sites.

Each room has recovered its $25–30 thousand initial investment in six to nine months due to savings in travel cost. Full-motion video has been used on an ad hoc basis for introducing new products, but it is felt that the possible gains from regular video conferencing do not justify the much higher costs at this time. Teleconference coordinators are employed to provide orientation sessions on teleconferencing procedures and equipment operation; schedule and maintain the rooms and equipment; charge users; and provide assistance when needed (Prem and Dray, 1984).

Video Conferencing

Except for some local, closed-circuit systems that require elaborate switching arrangements, at present seeing and being seen with full motion can occur at only two sites, although interactive audio can be established for all sites. One-way video—from the leader's location to all other locations—can be used when more than two sites are involved.

When we add the visual channel to audio conferencing, we have the most expensive and most difficult to orchestrate form of teleconferencing. On the other hand, we have the most realistic simulation of a face-to-face meeting, at least for two locations. The potential importance of this realism for regular problem-solving meetings will be discussed in the section on user reactions.

There is little question that video conferencing is a growth industry. Rosenthal reported in 1985 that the market for video teleconferencing has been growing at a 60 percent annual rate, and in 1986, Tyson reported: "According to *Quantum Science,* more than 210 video teleconferencing systems currently are in active use in the U.S. by some 75 companies" (p. 5). Dramatic reductions in transmission costs, including 60 percent off-hours discounts, are inducing many others to get on board. For example, a large, national chain of retail stores expects to begin operating a video network that will link some twenty-six cities by early 1987.

The major vendors of video conferencing rental facilities and implementation services include: American Satellite, AT&T's Picturephone Meeting Service, Hilton Hotels, Holiday Inns of America HI-NET service, Marriott Corporation, and Satellite Business Systems.

Computer Conferencing

A computer network provides only for message–graphics interaction, without audio and visual channels (unless a hybrid, double system is established). However, it provides a very important feature that the other forms of teleconferencing lack: inputs can be entered and read asynchronously, that is, in "nonreal" time.

All computers in the network can receive messages at any time. They then file and store them until local participants want to read them.

This means that conferees can participate at their convenience, provided the deadlines for decision making permit the conference to last more than an hour or two. This is quite advantageous when would-be participants cannot "meet" at the same time, when they are in widely varying time zones, or when they wish to reflect upon and/or do further research with regard to certain inputs before responding to them.

In addition, the stored file feature makes it feasible for members of the computer network to participate in several different conferences during the same period of time. For example, they can alternate their attention among several problems that need solutions. As long as all messages are properly addressed and filed, there is little danger of confusion. Kelleher and Cross (1985) report that the Institute of Nuclear Power Operators coordinates twenty to twenty-five ongoing computer conferences on various aspects of nuclear plant operation.

One must have software to run a computer conferencing system. Kelleher and Cross indicate that the following are the major systems available: Electronic Information Exchange System (EIES), operated by the New Jersey Institute of Technology; Infomedia Corporation's Notepad; Data Dynamics's GENeral Information Environment (Genie); Tymshare's Augment; and Cross Information Company's Matrix. They also discuss prices and special features of each.

An interesting applications example (Krembs, 1984) is provided by IBM's project to develop technical strategies via long-term, international computer conferencing by a group of widely dispersed professional employees. The conference started in March 1981 and by December 1981 had conferees in eighteen locations, including three abroad, with plans for nine more locations. Since each contribution was dated when filed, newcomers could easily catch up by reviewing the evolution of the documents in storage.

The conference was coordinated by a central administrator who set deadlines, solicited inputs from known experts, arranged audio teleconferences to resolve conflicts in opinion, and generally acted as managing editor of the evolving document. By September 1981, when the first comprehensive management review occurred, forty-five participants had taken part in fashioning eighty pages of integrated material.

User Reactions

Extensive research by the Communications Studies Group in England, involving hundreds of managers from business and government, indicates that we cannot generalize about the effectiveness of teleconferencing without relating the purpose of a meeting to the particular form of teleconferencing being used. Based on a comparison of face-to-face groups with audio conferencing and video conferencing groups, their research indicates that the chief role of visual cues from people is to communicate interpersonal attitudes. They are particularly important for getting to know others. For this purpose, face-to-face meetings are best, video conferencing is next best, audio conferencing follows, and (presumably) computer conferencing is the poorest.

Visual cues are relatively unimportant when we are engaged in cooperative problem solving with people we know. In fact, they are a handicap in that both audio and video teleconferences produce solutions as good as face-to-face meetings, in less time, and with more task orientation. However, face-to-face contacts at some point have proven to be indispensable, even in the most successful teleconferencing applications (Short, Williams, and Christie, 1976).

Birrell and White (1982) conducted additional studies for the U.S. Department of Defense, involving 191 middle and senior managers who solved problems in four-person groups via audio-only and video conferencing. The participants were asked to compare these modes with the face-to-face mode.

A strong majority felt that the two modes of teleconferencing were equal to or superior to the face-to-face mode with regard to task orientation, brevity, level of self-contribution, and friendliness. They felt that the two modes were equal to or superior to the face-to-face mode in stimulating colleague cooperation during cooperative problem solving, but not during competitive problem solving. However, they felt that the quality of discussion was significantly better for both types of problem solving under both types of teleconferencing.

There were two negative findings for audio-only teleconferencing: A majority felt that the face-to-face mode was equal to or superior to the audio-only mode with regard to "satisfaction"; and in response to a "helpfulness of equipment" question, a majority responded that the audio-only mode was "not helpful."

Two years later, Birrell and Young (1984) reported on more studies which compared face-to-face groups with audio conferencing and video conferencing groups. These confirmed earlier findings about teleconferences being briefer, more task-oriented, and equally productive in terms of good results; and, they added some additional findings. For both audio conferencing and video conferencing groups, Birrell and Young found that in comparison with face-to-face groups: (1) participants are less dogmatic and are more compromising; (2) participants are less confident about making judgments about others; (3) negotiation and bargaining are more objective in that the side with the strongest case is more likely to win; and (4) these effects, including shorter time requirements and greater task orientation, are generally stronger in the audio-only mode.

Although video conferencing is typically the most expensive form of teleconferencing, Boeing's local, microwave–transmission-based system, linking four of its main manufacturing plants in Northwest Washington State, is an exception. In 1982, in-house clients were paying only $52 per hour for full-motion, two-way color TV (Rathbun, 1983). A measure of the effectiveness of the system is provided by a report ("Videoconferencing . . . ," 1984) stating that the company completed development of its 757 model jetliner ahead of schedule because the network so facilitated collaboration on the part of executives, technicians, and pilots in making design decisions.

Computer Conferencing. Computer conferencing was not compared with the other forms of teleconferencing in the foregoing section because it was not included in the comparative studies we found. With the exception of the study reported below, we were unable to find systematically developed data. Nevertheless, survey and anecdotal results, coupled with dramatically expanding usage in an increasing number of organizations, strongly imply that it is a highly successful form of teleconferencing.

Hiltz, Johnson, Aronovitch, and Turoff (1980) compared the problem-solving performance of face-to-face groups and computer conferencing groups that used EIES System software. They found no difference in solution quality (as did the studies reported earlier for audio and video conference groups in comparison with face-to-face groups). In addition, they report that problems were viewed as being clearer by the computer conferencing groups in comparison with the face-to-face groups.

Some Observations. The findings reported above challenge the view that all forms of teleconferencing are inherently inferior to conventional, face-to-face meetings and that the only justification for going the electronic route is anticipated savings in travel expenses. It is clear that teleconferencing can provide other advantages. However, the extent to which these will be realized will depend upon several considerations. For instance, prior to teleconferencing, participants should have face-to-face opportunities to get acquainted. If this is not feasible, the initial teleconference should incorporate TV or "freeze-frame" visual channels. At least, photographs of all participants should be distributed, along with pertinent information about them. A leader should structure the conduct of the teleconference in ways that reflect the unique constraints and opportunities that exist. (INGT is particularly useful in this regard for the reasons discussed in the next section of this chapter.)

Based on focus-interview data obtained from audio teleconferees, Sherman (1984) finds that in audio-only conferences, participants should (1) identify themselves each time they speak, at least until they can clearly recognize each others' voices; (2) indicate when they have finished a given contribution, since pauses are often mistaken for endings; (3) acknowledge all queries that are directed to them personally, or to the group with at least a "yes" or "no" or "no comment" response. (Questioners tend to needlessly repeat themselves in the absence of feedback, feeling that no one is there, or that no one is listening.)

Role of INGT

The Improved Nominal Group Technique can contribute to problem-solving efficiency and effectiveness under all four forms of teleconferencing. INGT's premeeting collection and distribution of anonymous inputs will:

- Provide more and better inputs;
- Reduce teleconferencing expenses by providing a "beachhead" of twenty to thirty predigested contributions:
- Stimulate additional ideas for participants to input during the teleconference;
- Guide participants in preparing for the teleconference, in terms of both information gathering and reflective analysis; and
- Suggest additional individuals and resources to involve in the teleconference.

INGT's discussion guidelines assure orderly progress by controlling digressions, domination attempts, and needless repetition and argumentation, as they prevent premature evaluation and closure, while assuring equal participation opportunity to all. INGT's display and voting procedures will make it possible to get as close to the genuine, uncoerced positions of individual participants as one can get in a meeting situation.

We will now discuss how INGT's rules and procedures can be adapted to the specific characteristics of each of the four forms of teleconferencing.

Audio-Only Conferencing. Since there will be no graphics-transmission capability with audio-only conferencing, and inputting during the meeting will have to be done verbally, we will be able to realize the important benefits of anonymous inputting *only* during the premeeting phase of the conference. The leader should set a deadline for participants to mail their inputs to a "neutral address" so that a list of them can be prepared, duplicated, and returned to all before the conference begins.

There is another good reason for collecting premeeting inputs. During the conference, items must be inputted one at a time, verbally, and recorded by all participants as they are given. This imposes more of a coordination burden on the leader and probably requires more time than would use of a graphics-transmission system, since the use of separate telephone lines for the graphics and teleconferencing systems permits the inputting of new items and change proposals without suspending verbal interaction to discuss an item or to act upon a previous proposal. Using the graphics system, the leader still has to read all messages received (to verbally "display" them), but she or he can do this with the advantages of batching and of more convenient timing.

Since the leader will not be able to see a participant raise his or her hand to speak, another means of obtaining the floor must be used. One might say "Bill here, and I'd like to propose a change to an item." Or, during the discussion phase, when the leader asks if there is any comment on item #4, each person who wishes to comment about that item might say "So and so here, I'd like to comment." Then the leader can call upon each in an orderly manner. When a comment is completed, the participant should say something like "end," or "I'm finished" to avoid any confusion or interruptions during pauses. All participants should receive information about INGT before the conference and know what the discussion phase is for, and what it is *not* for.

Hopefully, there will be time for the first vote (and a second vote, if necessary) to be done by mail or express service to a "neutral address," so that voting can be anonymous.

Audio Conferencing with Graphics Transmission. The features of audio-only conferencing apply to this mode, except that the limitations on anonymous inputting and voting during the period of the conference are removed. Also, the requirement that premeeting inputs be collected and distributed by mail need not apply.

There are various types of equipment for transmitting inputs. Since the facsimile machine (FAX) is one of the most common means, we will refer to it to illustrate some written transmissions. First, assume that each teleconference location is equipped with a fast, Group 3 or 4 FAX and that the leader can tell when her or his machine is receiving, but need not know who dialed it.

The leader can initiate a card collection round at the beginning of the teleconference and during it by announcing that anyone who wants to input anonymously to his or her machine should do so at that point. FAX operation prevents voice transmission at the same time on a given phone line. If two or more teleconferees try to call the leader's FAX simultaneously, the sending machines that get a busy signal will hold and redial until the leader's FAX is free again. When the leader sees that the FAX has stopped receiving, he or she can announce the new inputs for all participants to add to their premeeting distribution list of items. In the same manner, ballots can be inputted quickly and anonymously.

The receiving process can be accelerated by having more than one FAX at the leader's location for the conferees to call, plus voice interactions need not be suspended during FAX transmissions if the FAX system is using telephone lines that are separate from the teleconferencing system.

Video Conferencing. When there are only two video conferencing sites involved, with two-way video permitting all conferees to see each other, the leader can coordinate comments in the same way as in a face-to-face INGT meeting. If there are more than two locations, permitting only one-way video *from* the leader's location, the leader will have to use the nonvideo adaptations discussed above.

Inputs should still be transmitted by FAX (or other non-TV graphics-transmission equipment), since the use of the video channel for this purpose would be both distracting and expensive. However, in addition to permitting conferees elsewhere to see the leader and other participants at her or his location, the one-way video arrangement makes possible the multiple transcription of multiple FAX-inputted contributions to multiple flipcharts for display to conferees at all locations. This will avoid the necessity of item-by-item dictation to these conferees, of new inputs, proposed changes to items, and voting results, as is required with nonvideo teleconferencing.

Computer Conferencing. Premeeting inputs can be collected by the deadline, numbered, and distributed with ease, all via the computer network. Since items, proposed changes, requests for clarification, and pros and cons about items are entered and read asynchronously (in "nonreal" time) during the conference, there is no real-time coordination problem for the leader. He or she has only to establish a schedule for entering each phase of INGT activity and then communicate appropriate deadlines for implementing each phase with appropriate timeliness.

For example, the leader announces a deadline for receipt of proposed changes to the premeeting list of inputs. Then the leader numbers and distributes these change proposals, indicating a deadline for objecting to any of them. If no objection to a particular change is "posted" by the deadline, the change is made.

The leader announces a deadline well in advance of the scheduled date for the first vote, by which time each participant is to communicate to the other participants any requests for clarification and pro and con statements she or he wishes to make about the various items on "display," referring to them by the numbers that were assigned by the leader. This process is repeated for any new items received. Then the anonymous first vote ballots are transmitted, participants examine the results, and then vote as to whether or not the discussion phase should be reopened in preparation for a second vote.

This discipline of formal inclusion and timely completion dates should help to prevent a negative consequence of asynchronous conferencing reported by conferees; namely, the tendency to lose participants along the way, as a computer conference fragments into small, private, interacting subgroups (See Vallee, 1986).

Due to its asynchronous nature, computer conferencing has the distinction of being the only medium for INGT that can reasonably accommodate several purposes (computer conferences) at the same time, whether they relate to identifying problems for different areas, solving various problems, reviewing specific documents, or a combination of these. As long as all transactions associated with a given conference (purpose) are labeled with that conference's unique code number, there should be no problem.

Computer conferencing provides another bonus: In addition to the permanent storage of the usual INGT materials (all inputs, approved changes to them, and voting tallies) all requests for clarification, responses to them, and pro and con comments about the display items are also automatically stored.

In Conclusion

Teleconferencing is here to stay. It is clear that the various forms of it are not just poor substitutes for a face-to-face meeting. They offer special advantages in their own right. They have passed the experimental stage and are prospering at an impressive rate. As technology continues to improve and costs continue to decline, this rate will increase.

The Improved Nominal Group Technique was designed to facilitate cooperative problem solving, and it has demonstrated its ability to do so admirably. Teleconferencing is particularly suited to this same purpose. When we combine the two properly, we achieve teleconferencing at its best.

Chapter Sixteen

Exploring Other Uses

There are two other areas in which the principles and procedures of the Improved Nominal Group Technique may have a productive impact: international relations and one-on-one relationships.

International Relations

In a workshop on the Middle East conflict, organized by Herbert Kelman, representatives of both sides of the issue became painfully aware of the dramatic differences in their perceptions of the same central "facts" (Armstrong, 1981). These opposing factions, like we Americans, are often appalled by the motives attributed to us by others, and surely others, at times, are appalled by what we attribute to them.

For example, many in the West assume that the only true interests of the Soviet government relate to the acquisition, preservation, and extension of power, both at home and abroad. But how much effort have Western authorities expended to check this out, including extended dialogue on the matter with the Soviets? For that matter, what consensus has been reached in Washington about our government's interests abroad, as opposed to the positions it has adopted? And what efforts have we made to acquaint the Soviets with our true interests?

Possible Role for INGT. Face-to-face meetings between parties who are antagonistic or suspicious of each other have a high potential for excessive arousal and interpersonal explosions, especially when the parties feel compelled to defend specific positions. But, as Fisher and Ury (1983) point out, when the emphasis shifts more to identifying and prioritizing each side's true interests, the need for either to dig in its heels on any given position is diminished, and the opportunity to search for new possibilities for mutual accommodation is enhanced.

INGT's premeeting phase should facilitate the generation of options for accommodating mutual interests through its provision of private brainstorming, anonymous inputting, and feedback of all inputs to each side for review and deliberation prior to face-to-face interaction.

INGT's discussion guidelines and its anonymous in-meeting inputting and complete display features have proved their ability to depersonalize sensitive items and to minimize interpersonal conflict. Consequently, there should be a higher probability of producing options to accommodate mutual interests that are attractive to both sides of a given situation.

These outputs could then be fashioned by either side, or by a neutral third party, into proposals to present to document review meetings for further refinement and problem identification by the parties and their respective consultants. This should be an efficient way to further operationalize Fisher and Ury's (1983) *One-Text, Principled-Negotiation* procedure that was used so successfully by President Carter in achieving the Camp David Accord between Egypt and Israel in 1978.

If one side resorts to "dirty tricks," Fisher and Ury suggest that the other side " . . . recognize the tactic, raise the issue explicitly, and question the tactic's legitimacy and desirability—negotiate over it." They go on to observe that "it will be easier to reform the negotiating process than to reform those with whom you are dealing" (1983, pp. 135, 136).

INGT-Enhanced Computer Conferencing. Based upon four years of EIES-based computer conferencing experience with some seven hundred conferees in the United States, Canada, and several foreign countries, Turoff and Hiltz (1984) discuss the possibilities of computer conferences for improving international relations. They point out that computer conferences provide a more inclusive and feasible basis for continuing interaction among numerous international conferees at various levels of influence. Further, the asynchronous (non–real-time) nature of computer conferencing affords the conferee time for translating messages; time for conferring with colleagues about, and reflecting upon, what is going on; and maximum flexibility during a crisis to respond to minute-by-minute developments, by being able to physically leave and reenter the conference without losing the continuity of developments. It also permits conferees to participate in many different conferences at the same time. In addition, newcomers can readily catch up with developments in any computer conference by reviewing the evolving message base in storage.

Computer conferencing also avoids some of the pitfalls of conventional face-to-face meetings. For instance, visual cues can be a liability in cross-cultural relations, since cultural differences often lead to misinterpretation. Computer conferees report seeing the same problems more clearly in comparison with face-to-face conferees. From an emotional standpoint, computer conferencing is a "cooler" medium that promotes a more positive, reflective atmosphere than face-to-face meetings. When faced with a human relations problem, computer conferees were more likely to decide upon solutions to save face and were less likely to decide upon negative-sanction solutions (for both parties) than were face-to-face conferees.

As discussed in Chapter Fifteen, we can enhance the effectiveness of a computer conference by utilizing the rules and procedures of the Improved Nominal Group Technique to conduct it. It is also important to have face-to-face, "get-acquainted" meetings for participants before a computer conference begins. If this is not feasible, then photographs of the conferees and pertinent information about them should be distributed in advance of the conference.

The combination of initial face-to-face meetings and continuing intercourse via computer conferencing—aided by a growing body of technical and interpersonal knowledge in computer memory—may well afford the best hope we have for improving international relations.

Enhancing One-On-One Relationships

Up to this point, our concern has been with group problem solving, but we can draw upon the same principles to enhance our one-on-one relationships.

Under normal, everyday circumstances, few people outside of our families (if even there) will give accurate feedback about behaviors we should try to change, for fear of offending us. And such restraint is practiced, in particular, by those over whom we have real power of reward or punishment. Consequently, we are often unaware of a need for change, or we have only a fuzzy notion of the exact change we should try to make.

Anonymous inputting provides a solution to this dilemma, and we don't have to have an INGT meeting to utilize it. We only have to place a locked box (with a slotted top) in a location where it cannot be monitored and ask subordinates to deposit their anonymous responses to questions like: "What do you feel I do well?" "What should I stop doing?" "What should I do differently?" "What should I start doing that I'm not doing?" "Is there anything else that bothers you that is not covered by the above?" Add the proviso: "As far as possible, please answer these questions in terms of specific, observable behaviors."

Some things may be easy to change, while others may be quite difficult. Well-entrenched habits die hard. We may find it useful to ask those we work with to signal us when we lapse into unwanted patterns.

Mutual Guidance and Support Group. Getting guidance and support from a *voluntary group* of associates who also want to improve their interpersonal skills can be especially helpful, as those who have participated in Dale Carnegie courses and Toastmasters International will confirm. The same questions presented above can be used. Anonymous responses are collected from all members about all other members and are then fed back to them.

No one should be prodded to seek help about suggested changes until he or she wants to. When someone does feel like it, she or he can ask the group for clarification and/or examples of each new target behavior. It is particularly helpful for a group member who is skilled with the new behavior or approach to demonstrate it through role playing. Then the "trainee" can practice what she or he has seen with another group member and get confirming or corrective feedback from the group.

By requesting that needs be expressed in terms of deficiencies in observable behavior, we help head off attempts to explore "what makes a person tick." Such attempts can be very threatening and counterproductive. By using aggregate anonymous inputting, we desensitize negative comments somewhat; thereby, helping group members to be more objective and supportive with each other.

The following features or implications of the INGT process can help supervisors in dealing with the work-related problems of individual subordinates. The following steps in the INGT process are especially useful:

1. State the problem without drawing any conclusions and, when needed, explain the requirements a solution must satisfy.
2. Solicit all relevant information before evaluating it.
3. Encourage collaborative problem solving.
4. Decide upon a specific plan of action.
5. Maintain the self-esteem of the subordinate while doing the above.

As is the case with problem-solving groups, adherence to these INGT-based principles will produce better solutions and greater understanding and commitment to them. It is the group leader's responsibility to reinforce this concept. It is unlikely that subordinates will perceive a supervisor as being arbitrary if he or she restricts any necessary unilateral diagnoses and prescriptions to those situations in which a subordinate is unresponsive to this collaborative approach.

Behavior Modeling Training. Training in behavior modeling provides the best means for mastering the application of these principles. It comprises:

1. *Instruction:* preferably via *learning points* that reflect sound knowledge.
2. *Demonstration Modeling:* preferably via video tapes of roleplays by respected, in-house leaders.
3. *Trainee Rehearsal:* with *feedback* from trainer and trainees as to compliance with the learning points.
4. *Effective Transfer to the Job:* via follow-up *refresher* and *remedial action meetings* and appropriate reinforcement for on-the-job implementation.

Instruction for dealing with individual, work-related problems is provided in learning point modules: Module 1, Nonjudgmental Information Gathering and Module 2, Remedial Action.

Ideally, *demonstration modeling* is provided by a video tape of a respected instructor or in-house leader in a roleplay which demonstrates all of the learning points. This provides uniform execution which can be viewed whenever needed without the presence of the model. However, a good live demonstration is equally effective.

Before *rehearsal,* trainees should view the modeling demonstration and write down (in the space on the right of the accompanying sheets) where each learning point occurs. If necessary, viewing of the modeling should be repeated until all learning points are properly identified.

Each trainee then role plays a supervisor in a realistic situation (preferably one submitted by the trainee) after being given a brief period to mentally rehearse how she or he will implement the learning points (displayed in the trainee's line of sight on a flipchart), while another trainee plays the subordinate. The trainee then receives feedback about compliance with the learning points and quality of execution.

Effective transfer is facilitated by follow-up meetings in which trainees can discuss and work through any problems they have encountered in trying to apply the learning points on the job. Maintenance of the new behavior is encouraged by improved relationships and, hopefully, by higher management recognition and support.

If it is not feasible to organize the type of program outlined above, one can still accomplish a great deal by practicing the learning points with a colleague or spouse, preferably, in the presence of an observer to provide feedback about how well the learning points are complied with. On the job, subordinates can be supplied with the learning points and asked to supply feedback, openly or anonymously.

The third learning point module is Module 3, Mediating Between Conflicting Individuals or Groups. It incorporates elements of both INGT and the method of Principled Negotiation developed at the Harvard Negotiation Project. It is as applicable to dealing with conflict between groups as it is to dealing with conflict between individuals.

*   *   *   *

Module 1. Nonjudgmental Information Gathering.

Explain specifically what you are concerned about and why you feel it is a problem. (Present any objective evidence you have, while withholding judgments of the person.)

(Indicate here places in video tape where learning points are modeled.)

Listen nonjudgmentally to give person full opportunity to explain events and/or feelings. (Usually, this requires no more than remaining silent and attentive after the first step; responding with short comments, such as: "I see," "Can you tell me more about such and such," and "What happened then?")

When there is much input, mirror what you have heard to check your understanding. (For example, "As I understand it, you did this because . . . [accurately play back what you have heard] or "You feel you have been unfairly accused, because . . . ")

When needed, set a specific date for a follow-up meeting. (The purpose of this meeting is to permit you to collect information from other sources and/or to prepare for a remedial action meeting.)*

Source: Developed by W. M. Fox.
Note: This module is to precede Module 2, Remedial Action.
*When use of this *Nonjudgmental Information Gathering* module leaves one or more problems to solve, continue your intervention with the *Remedial Action* module.

Module 2. Remedial Action.

If unknown to person, state conditions that a solution must satisfy.

Solicit and record person's ideas for solving problem, giving no evaluation of them. (Best to list ideas where both of you can see them, for example, on a flipchart or blackboard.)

Add your ideas—without evaluating them— then any additional ones which occur to either of you.

Discuss and evaluate the ideas in terms of pros and cons associated with each. (The choice of "no action" should be evaluated this way, also.)

*Seek agreement on a solution that states clear specific steps to be taken by either of you.**

Mirror back what other is committed to. (As a check on understanding, repeat the commitment, for example, say: "As I understand it, you will do such and such" [accurately playing back what you have heard].)

Agree on specific follow-up meeting or observation time and date. (The purpose here is to review progress or results.)

Praise person as soon as possible after successful implementation occurs. (Also give praise for completion of first step in a series of steps.)

(Indicate here places in video tape where learning points are modeled.)

Source: Developed by W. M. Fox.

Note: Precede this with Module 1, Nonjudgmental Information Gathering module when appropriate and deal with only one problem at a time.

*If you cannot agree and you have supervisory authority over person: *Specify action you will require, your reasons for requiring it, and when you expect it to occur.* (Then skip to second to last step: agreeing on specific follow-up time and date.)

Module 3. Mediating Between Conflicting Individuals or Groups.

I.   Get written commitment as to each party's willingness to search for resolution and to refrain from sharing data generated with nonparticipants (giving the latter assurance, yourself, in writing to both parties).

II.   Solicit written input from each participant as to
      A.   How I see other party
      B.   How I think other party sees me
      C.   How I see myself
      D.   What specific things (for an improved situation) other party should:
            1.   Start doing
            2.   Stop doing
            3.   Do differently (explain how)
            4.   Continue to do
                  (Be explicit, deal in terms of overt, observable behaviors for above categories as far as possible.)

III. Give all written input from each party to the other party, soliciting a written response as to
      A.   Things I will do (those things I just needed to be made aware of), indicating what, where, and when (if answers are not obvious)
      B.   Things I would like to do, but will need help with (specify help needed)
      C.   Things I feel are beyond my control to change (give reasons)
      D.   Things I am unwilling to change (give reasons)

IV.   In a meeting with both parties on neutral ground, display on flipchart pages:
      A.   What each has agreed to do (indicating what, where, and when if answers are not obvious)
      B.   What each would like to do if required help is given (specify help needed)
      C.   What each claims to have no control over (with reasons given)
      D.   What each is unwilling to change (with reasons given)

V.   Use INGT for IVB and IVC items (involving relevant others in the process), aiming for agreement as to who will do what, where, and when.

VI.   Use a Principled Negotiation approach for IVD items:
      A.   Get parties to agree to hear each other out (to permit ventilation of feelings) without interruption or debate. When a party is finished, have other party mirror or play back fully what has been said until presenter is satisfied with the accuracy of the representation.
      B.   Seek agreement on criteria (preferably objective) to be used for evaluating positions.
      C.   Have the parties explain the bases for, and the relative importance of, the interests they want to satisfy.

D.   Before a subsequent meeting, have the parties input, anonymously and in writing to you, all of the options they can think
of that will accommodate the interests of both parties in a
balanced way, as well as the estimated costs or risks to each
party of not altering each position.

E.   Duplicate and distribute the list of options and risks so the
parties will have the opportunity to reflect upon them and
formulate additional ideas to take to the meeting on 3 x 5
cards to input anonymously.

F.   Transcribe input from cards to flipchart pages for display
during meeting.

G.   Invite discussion of every option, giving parties the opportunity to seek clarification, and to talk for or against an option,
but not to argue or get personal.

H.   By means of a secret ballot, have the parties indicate which of
the options are acceptable to them. Have each party sign a
contract which specifies the who, what, where, and when of
agreed upon action.

I.   Agree upon a follow-up meeting date at which progress will
be evaluated.

If the parties agree, the entire procedure of Principled Negotiation
outlined above may be repeated for those issues which remain
unresolved, or the parties may agree to submit them to a mutually
acceptable arbitrator.

Positively reinforce agreed-upon new behaviors and progress toward
agreed-upon goals.

Source: Developed by W. M. Fox.

Chapter Seventeen

Concluding Remarks

We have seen why genuine participation in problem identification and problem solving is extremely valuable and why conventional group procedures tend to prevent or stifle participation. We have seen, also, how the problem is resolved by the proven elements of Improved Nominal Group Technique:

- Realistically-defined purpose,
- Assured anonymity for contributors,
- Productive individual premeeting activity,
- Complete display of inputs and changes made (which become permanent, inclusive briefing materials when the voting tally is added),
- Deferred evaluation,
- Assured opportunity for discussion,
- The second vote option,
- The document review meeting, and
- Discussion guidelines that encourage genuine participation while they conserve group time and effort.

We have reviewed INGT's unique capabilities for enhancing and maintaining the effectiveness of participation-based undertakings, such as

- Autonomous or self-managing work groups
- Bargaining teams

- Confrontation meetings
- Employee representation on boards
- Improshare
- Job redesign teams
- Management by objectives (MBO)
- Management of change teams
- Multiple management
- New design (greenfield) plants
- Organization development in the private sector
- Organization development in the public sector
- Program planning
- Project teams
- Quality circles
- Survey feedback programs
- Teleconferences
- Rucker plan
- Scanlon plan
- Venture teams

For all of the reasons presented in this book the Improved Nominal Group Technique (INGT) is superior to conventional procedures for identifying and evaluating options, positions, and problems; solving a problem; and debugging and refining a written proposal or other document.

1. *Your key responsibility as an INGT leader is to see that all participants comply strictly with INGT requirements.* Consequently, before leading a group with INGT, know the basics summarized in Chapters Four through Seven (and, if it's to be a document review meeting, Chapter Eight as well). Test yourself by taking the quiz that follows this section. This step is important, because new material has a way of being displaced by well-established habits when we go into action and come under fire.

2. *Do not test INGT with a hypothetical assignment.* INGT is a powerful tool, not a diversion. Use it only when participants have an authentic need to do so. Likely topics for a trial meeting are "What are the problems that interfere with our functioning?" Or, "How can we improve upon the way our unit is run?"

3. *Arrange for participants to read about INGT before the meeting.* Make sure all participants are briefed on the INGT procedures summarized in Chapter Ten (and Chapter Eight if it's to be a document review meeting) well in advance of the deadline for premeeting inputs.

4. *Get the group to agree to a fair trial.* INGT's strengths lie in its differences from conventional procedures, differences which will seem strange to many people. They will not be able to evaluate INGT properly until they have experienced it, and to experience it will require compliance with *all* of its requirements. Anything less will fall short of a fair test.

5. *Have participants evaluate the process.* After testing INGT fairly, ask participants to indicate anonymously on 3 x 5 cards how they compare it with what they've been doing.

We predict that when participants have experienced what the various parts of INGT can do, in combination, they will want to adopt the entire process. However, this is not mandatory, for each part contributes to better group process in its own right.

Cross-Cultural Applicability of INGT

How applicable are INGT's advantages to other cultures? The existence of markedly different perceptions across cultures about the legitimacy of the participative sharing of influence is well documented. Hofstede (1980) has shown that various nationals who work in similar positions for the same international firm have quite different views about such factors as *power distance* (the extent to which most of us should be dependent upon a few who will unilaterally make decisions that affect us) and *uncertainty avoidance* (the extent to which we consider deviant ideas dangerous and, therefore, feel we should conform and not question decisions). His results are based upon data obtained from some 116,000 individuals in forty countries and were further confirmed in a follow-up survey of 400 managers from different public and private organizations in various countries.

On the other hand, data from most of the same individuals of the same international firm—as well as thousands of others in different organizations and countries—indicated definite desire for greater participation, collaboration, and mutual responsiveness than these individuals felt they were getting. The same was found to be true for 800 priests and 200 supervisory and nonsupervisory nurses (Sirota, 1969; IDE Research Group, 1981; Carey, 1972; Alutto and Vredenburgh, 1977).

These findings point to two conclusions: (1) feelings about participative decision making (at least initially, before people have had successful experiences with it) vary significantly across cultures; and (2) most people across these same cultures want (even initially) more involvement in work-related decisions than their supervisors are giving them.

Both conclusions direct attention to the unique strengths of INGT. INGT procedures permit each group member to remain uninvolved or to become involved at a rate at which she or he is most comfortable, without being subject to coercion or embarrassment, as they maintain the assured opportunity for participation for each member. They help any leader willing to give them an honest trial to move his or her group toward genuine, more productive participation—regardless of the leader's background and experience—because they do most of the work. The chief constraint on the productive use of INGT *in any setting* will be an unwillingness to explore the benefits of shared influence.

So, here are the tools—grounded in years of research—that can help us to rise above our emotional and cognitive limitations. May we use them well, to enrich our personal, organizational, and community lives, and to improve our international relationships before it is too late.

Appendix

Test Your Understanding
of the Basics

All of the questions below deal with aspects of the Improved Nominal Group Technique (INGT) presented in this book. Before looking at the answers on page 173, *commit yourself* by getting a piece of paper and writing down your answer for each question. Then you will really know what you need to review.

Pick the *one* best answer for each of the following:

1. An INGT meeting is started with
   a. a silent writing period
   b. a card collection round
   c. could be either a or b; it depends
2. The leader conducts card collection rounds until
   a. all the cards are blank
   b. one-half of the cards are blank
   c. one-third of the cards are blank
3. INGT is suitable for a single group of up to
   a. five people
   b. nine people
   c. twenty people
   d. more than twenty people

4. Whai percent is used to determine the number of finalist items to have participants rank?
   a. 5%
   b. 10%
   c. 15%
   d. 30%

5. What is the *proper order* in which the following activities should occur? (1) discussion phase (2) card collection round (3) making a no-discussion proposal for change (4) the duplication and distribution of a list of inputs
   a. 1, 2, 3, 4
   b. 4, 2, 3, 1
   c. 4, 2, 1, 3
   d. 2, 1, 3, 4

Indicate *True* or *False* for the questions below. If you feel that any answer "depends upon something," state *what that is.*

6. Under no conditions should participants input blank cards.
7. INGT *requires* that a second vote be conducted.
8. Participants must remain in their seats until the meeting adjourns.
9. INGT does not permit the leader to input ideas.
10. A no-discussion proposal to change or drop an item requires a majority vote to be accepted.
11. *Alternation ranking* requires picking the most-preferred item first; then the least-preferred; the second most-preferred next; then the second least-preferred; and so on.
12. No-discussion proposals for change can be made only during the discussion phase of the meeting.
13. When a no-discussion proposal for changing the wording of an item is approved, a committee is automatically appointed to decide upon the new wording.
14. To get an item on display before the group, someone must propose the item, and it must be seconded by another.
15. Premeeting inputs should be transcribed to flipchart pages.
16. A display item should be eliminated or changed in such a way that it can still be read in its original form.

17. Each item should be critically evaluated as soon as it is put on display before the group.

18. Ony the leader should transcribe items to flipchart pages.

19. A secret ballot is used for voting: (1) when the leader feels that what is being voted on may be a sensitive issue for someone in the group, or (2) if a participant requests it.

20. Only *one objection* is required to keep an input from being put on display before the group.

21. The purpose of the discussion phase is to achieve group agreement about the value of each item.

22. The group is not required to discuss every item.

23. The author of an item on display is required to identify himself or herself at the request of any participant.

24. Participants should put cards on the table face up for a card collection round, so the leader can see whether or not they are blank.

25. A participant can input an item verbally.

26. A participant should be permitted to discuss an earlier item on the display list (that has already been discussed) whenever he wishes.

27. A participant is never permitted to repeat the same comments or observations about an item.

28. Arguing is permitted, as long as it doesn't get out of hand.

29. For the sake of neatness, the leader should see to it that all display sheets are removed and placed in a trash can at the end of a meeting.

30. The purpose of the silent writing period is to have participants prepare written evaluations of the items on display.

31. The best way to display inputs is either with flipchart pages or a sufficiently large blackboard.

32. All items on display must be numbered consecutively, from "1" up to the total number.

33. It is appropriate for a group to use INGT to identify and prioritize problems.

34. A majority vote is never sought by a leader using INGT.

35. It is the leader's job to take notes during the meeting for preparing minutes later.

36. All inputs should be kept on display throughout the entire meeting.

37. Items must be *printed* on the flipchart pages with letters which are at least three inches high.

38. One full-size flipchart stand with a full pad is sufficient for any INGT meeting.

39. Inputs should be edited for improved wording and grammatical errors when they are transcribed.

40. INGT makes no provision for *combining* items on display.

41. No comment is permitted on the part of a participant who makes a no-discussion proposal for change.

42. To save time and space, participants should include several ideas in a single input statement.

43. The leader should *restate* each no-discussion proposal for change before asking if there is any objection to it.

44. It is the leader's responsibility to enforce the requirements of INGT.

45. In ranking items (in voting), ties are not permitted by INGT.

46. The leader should reopen discussion on *all items* in preparation for a second vote.

47. Ranking is the only kind of voting permitted.

48. The leader should not express his or her opinion about an item during the discussion phase.

49. It is appropriate for a group to use INGT to solve a given problem.

50. It is *not* good practice to announce the established constraints that a solution must satisfy before the beginning of a meeting, because this will interfere with creativity.

51. INGT is more efficient when we can schedule several problems to be solved in the same meeting.

52. The deadline for premeeting inputs should be the starting time for the meeting.

53. Once premeeting inputs are solicited, no changes should be made concerning who is invited to attend the meeting.

54. The leader should enter approved no-discussion proposals for change on or by the items on display at the end of the meeting, just before the voting.

55. It is appropriate for a group to use INGT to identify and prioritize options or alternative opportunities.

56. It is appropriate to use INGT for making periodic reviews of existing rules, policies, and procedures to see if they are still needed or can be improved upon by the group.

57. It is appropriate to use INGT for group review of a written proposal.

58. INGT is appropriate for quality circles and autonomous work groups.

59. When the leaders of different INGT groups meet to compare and meld the voting results from their respective groups, they should use INGT for conducting the meeting.

60. INGT is appropriate for community program planning and other types of program planning.

61. No change is made final in a document review meeting until the completion of voting at the end of the meeting.

62. INGT can be used productively by bargaining teams.

63. INGT is an important tool for gathering information and building teams in organization development activity.

64. This book discusses procedures for melding the outputs of several groups working on the same assignment.

Answers to the Test Yourself Quiz

Before leading your first INGT meeting for identifying and prioritizing problems or for solving a problem, *you should be able to answer all these questions without error.* Page numbers are presented below with each answer, so you can easily review material for those you are not sure of or answer incorrectly. Review the missed questions right away. Make a list of their numbers so you can retest yourself on them later.

Before leading a document review meeting, you should review Chapter Eight in addition to being able to answer questions 1–54. Appropriate chapters should also be reviewed before using INGT for program planning and the other special applications discussed in the text.

1.   c. If participants had the opportunity to prepare cards in advance, the meeting starts with the leader conducting a card collection round; otherwise, it begins with the leader conducting a silent writing period (pages 44, 49, 50, 95).
2.   a. (pages 49, 54, 55, 96, 97).
3.   c. (pages 17, 82, 93). The answer may well be more than "20." We have experienced no problem with groups of twenty. But walk before you run. Don't experiment with larger groups until all participants are well experienced with INGT.
4.   c. (pages 61, 99).
5.   Of the answers listed, either b or c. Activity (4), the duplication and distribution of a list of inputs, is definitely *first* whenever it is possible to have premeeting inputting (pages 32, 43, 94). Activity (2), card collection round, is next. We collect all inputs before discussing their pros and cons (pages 49, 95, 97). Activity (1), the discussion phase, always follows activities (4) and (2) (pages 33, 55, 97). Activity (3), making a no-discussion proposal for change, *can occur anytime* after the first silent writing period at the beginning of the meeting until voting begins (pages 52, 57, 96).
6.   *False.* To *assure anonymous inputting,* we want a face down card from every participant for every card collection round; therefore, those who have nothing to input will have to submit blank ones. The leader continues to conduct periodic card collection rounds *until all cards are blank* (pages 49, 54, 55, 96, 97).
7.   *False.* A second vote is not required; it occurs only when a majority of group members see a need for it on the basis of first vote results (pages 61, 65, 100).
8.   *False.* When it is time to vote, the leader should urge participants who have any difficulty in reading the flipchart pages on the wall to go up to them and read them at close range (pages 62, 99).
9.   *False.* Leaders usually have much of value to contribute; however, they should avoid verbally inputting items for display (for the reasons discussed on pages 26, 59).
10.   *False.* A single objection—no explanation required—blocks a

no-discussion proposal for change from being adopted (pages 52, 96).

11. *True* (pages 61, 63).

12. *False.* No-discussion proposals for change can be made at any time after the first silent writing period at the beginning of the meeting up to the time voting begins (pages 40, 52, 57, 96).

13. *False.* The proposer *alone* is responsible for presenting the desired wording at the time he or she makes the proposal (pages 52, 53).

14. *False. All inputted items are displayed.* No approval is required. Premeeting inputs are displayed via a typed and duplicated list, and items inputted at the meeting are transcribed to flipchart pages for display (pages 40, 49, 52, 95, 96).

15. *False.* They are displayed via typed, duplicated lists. The leader should have extra copies to distribute at the meeting to any participant without one in hand (pages 43-44, 52, 97-98).

16. *True* (page 53).

17. *False.* It is extremely important to *avoid* premature evaluation (for the reasons discussed on pages 33, 49, 97). We should have *all* inputs on display (via a duplicated list of premeeting inputs and flipchart pages of in-meeting inputs) before any are evaluated.

18. *False.* When a card collection round produces many items to transcribe to flipchart pages, the leader should solicit help from other group members or secretarial assistants (see pages 51-52, 95 for details).

19. *False.* A secret ballot should be used for *all* first and second votes and any subsequent voting (for the reasons presented on pages 40-41).

20. *False.* This applies to a proposed change of an item on display; only one objection is required to block the change being made. However, the proposer of a blocked no-discussion proposal for change *needs no one's approval to add the changed item to the display.* All items which are inputted, anonymously or verbally, before the meeting or during the

meeting, are put on display before the group throughout the entire meeting (pages 40, 49, 52, 95–96).

21. *False.* The purpose of the discussion phase is to provide all participants with the opportunity to seek or give clarification as to what an item means or implies and to present pros or cons about an item (pages 39, 56, 97).

22. *True.* The leader's responsibility is only to assure the opportunity for everyone, *not* to require discussion or to try to see a need for it (pages 37, 56–57, 97).

23. *False.* Just the opposite, *we want to play down authorship.* The author of an item on display may volunteer to identify herself or himself, but the leader should promptly rule as out of order any attempt to seduce or coerce this information from the group or from any group member (pages 39, 56, 58, 93).

24. *False.* The leader should insist that cards be inputted facedown to guarantee the anonymity of inputting (pages 49, 51, 55, 95).

25. *True* (pages 54, 56, 57, 59, 97). However, verbal inputting should not be encouraged or accepted as a group norm or desired behavior by a group committed to INGT (for the reasons presented on pages 23–29).

26. *True.* INGT is designed and intended to facilitate constructive discussion, not to inhibit it (pages 57, 97).

27. *False.* Repetition is permitted whenever someone (other than the presenter) expresses a need for it (pages 56, 59, 97).

28. *False.* A key goal of INGT is to facilitate constructive discussion by minimizing browbeating, personality clashes, and appeals to emotion in place of reason: arguments, debates, and hard sells are out of order (pages 56, 57, 97).

29. *False* (pages 70, 101). Display sheets should be carefully rolled and stored. They provide an invaluable record of group action (for the uses discussed on pages 70, 101, 125–126).

30. *False.* The purpose of the silent writing period is to provide participants with a distraction-free climate for writing contributions on 3 x 5 cards to input anonymously in the next card collection round (pages 50, 96).

31. *False.* Only something like flipchart pages provide a permanent, transportable record of group action and, more times than not, enough space to display the items inputted during a meeting (pages 48, 70).

32. *False.* This would be particularly cumbersome when we want several people to transcribe at the same time to prevent a large number of inputted items from becoming a time-consuming bottleneck to group progress. The only requirement is that each item have a different numerical identity: one transcriber can number items 1A, 2A, 3A; another 1B, 2B, 3B; and so on (pages 51, 52).

33. *True* (pages 30, 43, 60, 94).

34. *False.* The leader should use a majority vote to decide the following: (1) setting a time limit on discussion of any given item, agreeing to go beyond a scheduled stopping time, or agreeing to an additional meeting in the face of insufficient time relative to the number or items to be considered (pages 55-56, 97); (2) when an additional vote is needed (pages 65-66, 100); (3) choosing a solution to a problem from among finalist alternatives (pages 60-61); and (4) whether or not each proposed change to a document that was blocked by an objection should be adopted (page 80).

35. *False.* The premeeting input list (with approved changes noted) and the completed flipchart pages (including the voting tally) provide all the information that will be needed to prepare minutes later, should they be desired (page 70). We feel that the display materials (accompanied by explanation tailored to the listener's knowledge of INGT procedures) provide the most effective means for briefing others about group action.

36. *True* (pages 33-36, 52).

37. *False.* All we need is for items to be transcribed so that they can be read from every participant's seat (page 48).

38. *False.* In most cases, we will experience a transcribing bottleneck if we have only one flipchart. It is wise to have three of them set up, ready for use (pages 48, 51, 95).

39. *False.* They should not be rewritten (for the reasons given on page 50). However, superfluous words or phrases may be

dropped to conserve time and space. But if in doubt, do not leave anything out.

40. *False.* A no-discussion proposal for change can be used to combine items (pages 52–53, 96). However, the leader should discourage any movement toward seeing how many items *can* be combined, stressing the need to avoid unduly restricting choices for voting, and reminding the group that the "15 percent rule" will adjust the number of items to be ranked to reflect the number on display.

41. *False* (pages 40, 52, 96). However, comments are limited to reasons for making the no-discussion proposal for change; for example: "I feel that item #8 should be eliminated because it is so similar to #15," or "I feel that the meaning of #3 will be clearer if we change such and such a word or phrase," or "I think items 2 and 12 should be combined because they deal with highly interrelated aspects of the same issue." Extended description or discussion of the inadequacies of an item or presentation of pros and cons is out of order.

42. *False.* Different ideas should be stated in separate input statements (although several statements may be written on the same input card) (pages 51–53). When the first vote is conducted, it is better to err in the direction of too many choices rather than too few (due to the excessive lumping of ideas into one item). Voters will be free to ignore any items they wish and the number to be ranked is adjusted for the number on display, so there is really little danger of having too many.

43. *True* (pages 53, 96). If the proposal for change is lengthy, it should be written on a flipchart for all to read in addition to being stated by the leader. It is essential that every participant know exactly to what he or she is being asked to respond.

44. *True* (pages 57–58, 97, 166). This is the leader's *most important* function.

45. *False.* (Details on handling ties are presented on pages 61–62).

46. *False.* Discussion is reopened on only a subset of items which

received higher rank scores (as discussed on pages 65–66, 100).

47. *False*. (See answer to question 34 and the discussion of other approaches on pages 67–70.) We feel that for identifying and prioritizing problems (and for reducing a large number of proposed solutions to a more manageable subset, from which a solution can be picked via majority vote) ranking, when used with the second vote option, is hard to improve upon (for the reasons discussed on pages 66–67).

48. *False*. But the leader should avoid any appearance of trying to sell or impose a position (for the reasons discussed on page 59).

49. *True* (pages 30, 43, 60, 94).

50. *False* (pages 31–32, 45, 94). To avoid wasting time and effort, it is necessary for participants to know what constraints a solution must satisfy.

51. *False* (pages 30, 44, 94). We should deal with one problem at a time to be sure we do justice to it in terms of time and attention (keeping in mind that one problem may actually represent several closely interrelated, smaller problems).

52. *False*. We need adequate time to type, duplicate, and distribute a list of the premeeting inputs, and we need time for participants to study the list, formulate proposed changes to it, and prepare additional input cards suggested by it *before* the meeting (as discussed on pages 32–33, 43, 94–95).

53. *False* (page 33). Premeeting inputs often prompt us to invite to a meeting people whom we otherwise would not have thought of including.

54. *False* (pages 53, 58, 96). All changes should be entered on or by the items in question at the time they are approved (that is, if no one objects to the change).

55. *True* (pages 30, 43, 94).

56. *True* (recognizing that the document review meeting is the form of INGT that we use in such cases, pages 30, 43, 78, 94).

57. *True* (pages 30, 43, 94).

58. *True* (pages 110–111, 119–120).

59. *False*. INGT is *not* appropriate for this type of meeting (page 82).

60. *True* (recognizing the special considerations presented on pages 84–91).

61. *False.* If a change is not objected to, it is immediately adopted and entered on or by the item in question on the flipchart or premeeting distribution list (page 79).

62. *True* (pages 122–124).

63. *True* (pages 128, 138–139, 157–158). The importance of anonymity for effective problem identification is discussed on pages 23–25.

64. *True* (pages 82–84).

References

Ackoff, R. L. *A Concept of Corporate Planning.* New York: Wiley, 1970.

Alutto, J. A., and Vredenburgh, D. J. "Characteristics of Decisional Participation by Nurses." *Academy of Management Journal,* 1977, *20,* 341–347.

Arbose, J. "Is Worker Democracy Working?" *International Management,* Nov. 1979, pp. 14–18.

Argyris, C. "Interpersonal Barriers to Decision Making." *Harvard Business Review,* Mar.–Apr. 1966, pp. 84–97.

Armstrong, B. "Herbert Kelman: Reducing Conflict to a Science." *APA Monitor,* Jan. 1981, pp. 5, 55.

Arrow, K. *Social Choice and Individual Values.* Cowles Commission Monograph, no. 12. New York: Wiley, 1951.

Beckhard, R. "The Confrontation Meeting." *Harvard Business Review,* Mar.–Apr. 1967, pp. 149–155.

Beckhard, R., and Harris, R. T. *Organizational Transitions: Managing Complex Change.* Reading, Mass.: Addison-Wesley, 1977.

Birrell, J. A., and White, P. N. "Using Technical Intervention to Behavioural Advantage." *Behaviour and Information Technology,* 1982, *1,* 305–320.

Birrell, J. A., and Young, I. "Teleconferencing and Long-Term Meeting: Improving Group Decision Making." In L. Parker and C. Olgren (eds.), *The Teleconferencing Resource Book.* New York: Elsevier Science, 1984.

BNA Films. *The New Truck Dilemma.* Washington, D. C.: Bureau of National Affairs, 1965.

Borda, J. C. "Mémoire sur les election au scrutin" [Treatise on Balloting], in *Historie de l'académie royale des science.* (Originally published 1781.) As reported by R. A. Chechile, in W. C. Swap and Associates (eds.), *Group Decision Making.* Beverly Hills, Calif.: Sage, 1984.

Bragg, J., and Andrews, I. "Participative Decision Making: An Experimental Study in a Hospital." *The Journal of Applied Behavioral Science,* 1973, *9,* 727-735.

Carey, R. G. "Correlates of Satisfaction in the Priesthood." *Administrative Science Quarterly,* 1972, *17,* 185-195.

Chechile, R. A. "Logical Foundations for a Fair and Rational Method of Voting." In W. C. Swap and Associates (eds.), *Group Decision Making.* Beverly Hills, Calif.: Sage, 1984.

Coch, L., and French, J.R.P. "Overcoming Resistance to Change." *Human Relations,* 1948, *1,* 512-532.

Cole, R. E. "Learning from the Japanese: Prospects and Pitfalls." *Management Review,* 1980, *9,* 22-25.

Condorcet, M. *Essai sur l'application de l'analyse à la probabilité des décisions rendues à la pluralite des voix* [Essay on the Application of Analysis to the Probability of Majority Decisions]. (Originally published 1785.) As reported by R. A. Chechile, in W. C. Swap and Associates (eds.), *Group Decision Making.* Beverly Hills, Calif.: Sage, 1984.

Cotton, J. L., and others. "Rethinking Employee Participation: A Multidimensional Perspective and Review." Paper presented at annual meeting of the Academy of Management, San Diego, Calif., Aug. 1985.

Cowan, R. *Teleconferencing: Maximizing Human Potential.* Reston, Va.: Reston Publishing, 1984.

Dalkey, N., and Helmer, O. "An Experimental Application of the Delphi Method to the Use of Experts." *Management Science,* 1963, *9,* 458-464.

Dearborn, D., and Simon, H. A. "Selective Perception: A Note on the Departmental Identification of Executives." *Sociometry*, 1958, *21*, 140–144.

Delbecq, A. L., and Van de Ven, A. H. "A Group Process Model for Problem Identification and Program Planning." *The Journal of Applied Behavioral Science*, 1971, 7, 466–492.

Delbecq, A. L., Van de Ven, A.. H., and Gustafson, D. H. *Group Techniques for Program Planning: A Guide to Nominal Group and Delphi Processes*. Glenview, Ill.: Scott, Foresman, 1975.

Dodd, W. E., and Pesci, M. L. "Managing Morale Through Survey Feedback." *Business Horizons*, June 1977, 36–45.

Driscoll, J. W. "Working Creatively With a Union: Lessons From the Scanlon Plan." In M. Beer and B. Spector (eds.), *Readings in Human Resource Management*. New York: Free Press, 1985.

Fein, M. *Improshare: An Alternative to Traditional Managing*. Norcross, Ga.: Institute of Industrial Engineers, 1981.

Fein, M. *Improved Productivity Through Worker Involvement*. Hillsdale, N.J.: Mitchell Fein, 1982.

Fischhoff, B., Slovic, P., and Lichtenstein, S. "Fault Trees: Sensitivity of Estimated Failure Probabilities to Problem Representation." *Journal of Experimental Psychology: Human Perception and Performance*, 1978, *4* (2), 330–344.

Fisher, R., and Ury, W. *Getting to Yes*. New York: Penguin Books, 1983.

Fleishman, E. A. "Attitude Versus Skill in Work Group Productivity." *Personnel Psychology*, 1965, *18*, 253–266.

Fox, W. M. "Group Reaction to Two Types of Conference Leadership." *Human Relations*, 1957, *10*, 279–289.

Fox, W. M. "Compensation, Special Plans." In L. R. Bittel and M. A. Bittel (eds.), *Encyclopedia of Professional Management*. New York: McGraw–Hill, 1978.

Frankenhauser, M., and Gardell, B. "Underload and Overload in Working Life: Outline of a Multidisciplinary Approach." *Journal of Human Stress*, September, 1976.

French, W. L., and Bell, C. H., Jr. *Organization Development: Behavioral Science Interventions for Organization Improvement*. (3rd ed.) Englewood Cliffs, N.J.: Prentice–Hall, 1984.

Frost, C. F. "The Scanlon Plan: Anyone for Free Enterprise?" *MSU Business Topics*, 1978, *26* (1), 25–33.

Frost, C., Wakeley, J., and Ruh, R. *The Scanlon Plan for Organization Development: Identity, Participation, and Equity.* East Lansing: Michigan State University Press, 1974.

Glass, D. C., Singer, J. E., and Friedman, L. N. "Psychic Cost of Adaptation to an Environmental Stressor." *Journal of Personality and Social Psychology,* 1969, *12,* 200–210.

Golembiewski, R. T. *Humanizing Public Organizations.* Mt. Airy, Maryland: Lomond Publications, 1985.

Goodman, P. S. "Quality of Work Projects in the 1980's." *Labor Law Journal,* Aug. 1980, 487–494.

Guetzkow, H., and Gyr, J. "An Analysis of Conflict in Decision-Making Groups." *Human Relations,* 1954, *7,* 367–382.

Gustavsen, B., and Humnius, G. "Industrial Relations in Norway." *New Zealand Journal of Industrial Relations,* 1981, *6,* 125–138.

Guzzo, R. A. "I/O Psychology and Productivity: A Matter of Recognition?" *The Industrial-Organizational Psychologist,* 1984, *24* (2), 20–23.

Hackman, R., Jr., and Oldham, G. R. *Work Redesign.* Menlo Park, Calif.: Addison-Wesley, 1980.

Hammond, K. R., and Adelman, L. "Science, Values and Human Judgment." *Science,* 1976, *194,* 389–396.

Hare, A. P. *Handbook of Small Group Research.* (2nd ed.) New York: Free Press, 1976.

Hedberg, B., Nystrom, P., and Starbuck, W. "Camping on Seesaws: Prescriptions for a Self-Designing Organization." *Administrative Science Quarterly,* 1976, *21,* 41–65.

Henry, E. R. "Establishing Yardsticks." *Social Science Research Reports.* New York: Standard Oil Company, 1962, vol. 1, pp. (1-3.01-1)–(1-3.01-7).

Hilgendorf, E. L., and Irving, B. L. "Workers Experience of Participation: The Case of British Rail." *Human Relations,* 1976, *29,* 471–505.

Hill, R. "Working on the Scanlon Plan." *International Management,* Oct. 1974, pp. 39–43.

Hiltz, S. R., Johnson, K., Aronovitch, C., and Turoff, M. *The Effects of Computerized Conferencing vs. Face to Face Modes of Communication on the Process and Outcome of Group Deci-*

sion Making: A Controlled Experiment. Research Report, no. 11. Newark: New Jersey Institute of Technology, Computerized Conferencing and Communications Center, 1980.

Hinrichs, R., Jr. *Practical Management for Productivity.* New York: Van Nostrand Reinhold, 1978.

Hofstede, G. "Motivation, Leadership, and Organization: Do American Theories Apply Abroad?" *Organizational Dynamics,* 1980, *9* (1), 42–63.

Huber, G. P., and Delbecq, A. "Guidelines for Combining the Judgments of Individual Members in Decision Conferences." *Academy of Management Journal,* 1972, *15,* 161–174.

IDE Research Group. *Industrial Democracy in Europe.* Oxford, England: Claredon Press, 1981.

Imberman, W. "Why Quality Circles Don't Work." *Canadian Business,* 1982, *20* (11), 24–27.

Ingle, S. *Quality Circles Master Guide.* Englewood Cliffs, N.J.: Prentice-Hall, 1982.

Ivancevich, J. M. "An Analysis of Participation in Decision Making Among Project Engineers." *Academy of Management Journal,* 1979, *22,* 253–269.

Janis, I. L. *Victims of Groupthink.* Boston: Houghton Mifflin, 1972.

Johnson, D., Maruyama, G., Johnson, R., and Nelson, D. "Effects of Cooperative, Competitive, and Individualistic Goal Structures on Achievement: A Meta-Analysis." *Psychological Bulletin,* 1981, *89,* 63–100.

Kanter, R. M. *The Change Masters.* New York: Simon & Schuster, 1983.

Karasek, R. A. "Job Socialization and Job Strain: The Implications of Two Related Psychosocial Mechanisms for Job Design." In B. Gardell and G. Johansson (eds.), *Man and Working Life: A Social Science Contribution to Work Reform.* New York: Wiley, 1981.

Kelleher, K., and Cross, T. *Teleconferencing: Linking People Together Electronically.* Englewood Cliffs, N.J.: Prentice-Hall, 1985.

Krembs, G. M. "Strategic Planning Via International Computer

Conferencing." In L. Parker and C. Olgren (eds.), *The Teleconferencing Resource Book.* New York: Elsevier Science, 1984.

Kushell, E. "Quality Circle Failures: Reasons, Analyses, and an Alternative." Paper presented at National Conference of Human Resources Management and Organizational Behavior, Denver, Feb. 24–27, 1985.

Latham, G., and Saari, L. "The Importance of Supportive Relationships in Goal Setting." *Journal of Applied Psychology,* 1979, *64,* 163–168.

Lau, A., Newman, A., and Broedling, L. "The Nature of Managerial Work in the Public Sector." *Public Administration Review,* 1980, *40,* 513–520.

Lawler, E. E. "Leadership in Participative Organization." In J. G. Hunt, D. M. Hosking, C. A. Schriesheim, and R. Stewart (eds.), *Leaders and Managers: International Perspectives on Managerial Behavior and Leadership.* New York: Pergamon Press, 1984.

Lawler, E. E. *High-Involvement Management: Participative Strategies for Improving Organizational Performance.* San Francisco: Jossey-Bass, 1986.

Lawler, E. E., Renwick, P. A., and Bullock, R. J. "Employee Influence on Decisions: An Analysis." *Journal of Occupational Behavior,* 1981, *2,* 115–123.

Lawrence, P. R., and Dyer, D. *Renewing American Industry.* New York: Free Press, 1983.

Likert, R. *New Patterns of Management.* New York: McGraw-Hill, 1961.

Likert, R. "Human Resource Accounting: Building and Assessing Productive Organizations." *Personnel,* May–June 1973, pp. 8–24.

Likert, R., and Likert, J. *New Ways of Managing Conflict.* New York: McGraw-Hill, 1976.

Long, R. J. "Introducing Employee Participation in Ownership and Decision Making." In J. B. Cunningham and T. H. White (eds.), *Quality of Working Life.* Ottawa: Canadian Government Publishing Centre, 1984.

McClelland, D. C. "The Two Faces of Power." *Journal of International Affairs,* 1970, *24,* 29–47.

MacKinnon, W. J., and Anderson, L. "The SPAN III Computer Program for Synthesizing Group Decisions: Weighting Participants' Judgments in Proportion to Confidence." *Behavior Research Methods and Instrumentation,* 1976, *8,* 409–410.

McMahon, J. T. "Participative and Power-Equalized Organizational Systems." *Human Relations,* 1976, *29,* 203–214.

McMurry, F. "Report on the Reliability of the Alternation Ranking Technique." *Social Science Research Reports.* Newark, N.J.: Standard Oil Company, 1963, vol. 3, pp. (3-7.15-1)–(3-7.15-4).

Madsen, D. B., and Finger, J. R., Jr. "Comparison of Written Feedback Procedure, Group Brainstorming, and Individual Brainstorming." *Journal of Applied Psychology,* 1978, *63,* 120–123.

Maier, N.R.F. "Assets and Liabilities in Group Problem-Solving: The Need for an Integrative Function." *Psychological Review,* 1967, *74,* 239–249.

Maier, N.R.F., and Hoffman, L. "Group Decision in England and the United States." *Personnel Psychology,* 1962, *15,* 75–87.

Maier, N.R.F., and Verser, G. C. *Psychology in Industrial Organizations.* Boston: Houghton Mifflin, 1982.

Mann, F., and Dent, J. "Appraisals of Supervisors and Attitudes of Their Employees in an Electric Power Company." Ann Arbor, Mich.: Institute for Social Research, 1954.

Manz, C. C., and Sims, H., Jr. "The Potential for 'Groupthink' in Autonomous Work Groups." *Human Relations,* 1982, *35,* 773–784.

Manz, C. C., and Sims H. P. "Searching for the 'Unleader': Organizational Member Views on Leading Self-Managing Groups." *Human Relations,* 1984, *37,* 409–424.

Marrow, A., Bowers, D., and Seashore, S. *Management by Participation.* New York: Harper & Row, 1967.

Marrow, A., and French, J.R.P. "Changing a Stereotype in Industry." *Journal of Social Issues,* 1945, *1,* 33–37.

Mason, R. O., and Mitroff, I. I. *Challenging Strategic Planning Assumptions.* New York: Wiley-Interscience, 1981.

Mento, A. J. "Demystifying the Mystique of Quality Circles." In D. Ray (ed.), *Contribution of Theory and Research to the*

Practice of Management. State College: Southern Management Association, Mississippi State University, 1982.

"A Methodology for Participative Formulation of Government Policies and Programs for Small Business." *American Journal of Small Business,* 1979, *4,* 39-54.

Milgram, S. "Some Conditions of Obedience and Disobedience to Authority." *Human Relations,* 1965, *18,* 57-76.

Miller, G. A. "The Magical Number Seven, Plus or Minus Two: Some Limits on Our Capacity for Processing Information." *Psychological Review,* 1956, *63,* 81-97.

Miner, J. B. *Theories of Organizational Behavior.* Hinsdale, Ill.: Dryden Press, 1980.

Miner, J. B. *Theories of Organizational Structure and Process.* Hinsdale, Ill.: Dryden Press, 1982.

Mintzberg, H. *The Nature of Managerial Work.* Englewood Cliffs, N.J.: Prentice-Hall, 1973.

Mohrman, S. "A New Look at Participation in Decision Making: The Concept of Political Access." In R. C. Huseman (ed.), *Academy of Management Proceeding '79.* Athens: University of Georgia, 1979.

Moore, B. E., and Ross, T. L. *The Scanlon Way to Improved Productivity: A Practical Guide.* New York: Wiley, 1978.

Neider, L. L. "An Experimental Field Investigation Utilizing an Expectancy Theory View of Participation." *Organizational Behavior and Human Performance,* 1980, *26,* 425-442.

Nightingale, D. V. " 'Continuous Renewal': Lessons from a QWL Project." In J. B. Cunningham and T. H. White (eds.), *Quality of Working Life.* Ottawa: Canadian Government Publishing Centre, 1984.

Nutt, P. C. "Field Experiments Which Compared the Effectiveness of Design Methods." *Decision Sciences,* 1976, *7,* 739-758.

Nutt, P. C. "An Experimental Comparison of the Effectiveness of Three Planning Methods." *Management Science,* 1977, *23,* 499-511.

O'Boyle, T. F. "Loyalty Ebbs at Many Companies as Employees Grow Disillusioned." *Wall Street Journal,* July 11, 1985.

Ouchi, W. G. *Theory Z: How American Business Can Meet the Japanese Challenge.* Reading, Mass.: Addison-Wesley, 1981.

Parnes, S. J. "The Literature of Creativity (Part II)." *Journal of Creative Behavior,* 1967, *1,* 191–240.

Peters, T. J., and Waterman, R. H., Jr. *In Search of Excellence.* New York: Harper & Row, 1982.

Prem, D. C., and Dray, S. M. "Teleconferencing at Honeywell." In L. Parker and C. Olgren (eds.), *The Teleconferencing Resource Book.* New York: Elsevier Science, 1984.

Rathbun, R. D. "Teleconferencing Applications." In E. A. Lazer (ed.), *The Teleconferencing Handbook.* White Plains, N.Y.: Knowledge Industry Publications, 1983.

Rosenberg, R. D., and Rosenstein, E. "Participation and Productivity: An Empirical Study." *Industrial and Labor Relations Review,* 1980, *33,* 355–367.

Rosenthal, B. E. "Teleconferencing Grows." *Dun's Business Month,* Jan. 1985, p. 96.

Sadler, P., and Hofstede, G. "Leadership Styles: Preferences and Perceptions of Employees of an International Company in Different Countries." *Mens en Onderneming* [People in Business], 1972, *26,* 43–63.

Samuel, Y. *Social Consensus and Social Change: A Study of Groups in Complex Organizations.* Technical Report. Ann Arbor, Mich.: Institute for Social Research, University of Michigan, Aug. 1972.

Schweiger, D. M., Sandberg, W. R., and Ragan, J. W. "Group Approaches for Improving Strategic Decision Making: A Comparative Analysis of Dialectical Inquiry, Devil's Advocacy, and Consensus." *Academy of Management Journal,* 1986, *29,* 51–71.

Schwenk, C. R. "Information, Cognitive Biases, and Commitment to a Course of Action." *Academy of Management Review,* 1986, *11,* 298–310.

Scott, R. C. *Incentives in Manufacturing: A Critical Review of Individual and Plantwide Programs in Current Use.* Cambridge, Mass.: Eddy-Rucker-Nickels Co. (Series of articles originally published 1965, in Mar.–Dec. issues of *Circuits Manufacturing Magazine*)

Seelye, H. N., and Sween, J. A. "Critical Components of Successful U. S. Quality Circles." *The Quality Circle Journal,* 1983, *6* (1), 14–17.

Shaw, M. E. *Group Dynamics.* New York: McGraw–Hill, 1976.

Sherman, V. S. "Learning from Experience: Some User Reactions to Teleconferencing." In L. Parker and C. Olgren (eds.), *The Teleconferencing Resource Book.* New York: Elsevier Science, 1984.

Short, J., Williams, E., and Christie, B. *The Social Psychology of Telecommunications.* New York: Wiley, 1976.

Simmons, J., and Mares, W. *Working Together.* New York: Knopf, 1983.

Sirota, D. "International Survey of Job Goals and Beliefs." *Proceedings of the Sixteenth International Congress of Applied Psychology.* Amsterdam, Swets and Zeitlinger, 1969.

Smith, F. J. "Case Study: Motivation." In *Proceedings of the Productivity Conference.* Chicago: National Commission on Productivity—Region V, 1972.

Stokes, B. "Answered Prayers." *MBA,* Dec. 1978/Jan. 1979, pp. 12–23.

Sullivan, J. J. "An Experimental Study of a Method for Improving the Effectiveness of the Nominal Group Technique." Unpublished doctoral dissertation, Department of Management, University of Florida, 1978.

TeleSpan Newsletter, June 15, 1983, vol. 3, p. 6.

Thorsrud, E. "Policy-Making as a Learning Process in Working Life." In B. Gardell and G. Johansson (eds.), *Man and Working Life: A Social Science Contribution to Work Reform.* New York: Wiley, 1981.

Thorsrud, E. "The Scandinavian Model: Strategies of Organizational Democratization." In B. Wilpert and A. Sorge (eds.), *International Yearbook of Organizational Democracy.* Vol. 2 *International Perspectives on Organizational Democracy.* New York: Wiley, 1984.

Tichy, N. M., and Nisberg, J. N. "When Does Work Restructuring Work? Organizational Innovations at Volvo and G.M." *Organizational Dynamics,* 1976, *5* (1), 63–80.

Torrance, E. P. "Some Consequences of Power Differences on Decision-Making in Permanent and Temporary Three-Man Groups." In A. P. Hare, E. F. Borgatta, and R. F. Bales (eds.), *Small Groups.* New York: Knopf, 1955.

Torrance, E. P. "Group Decision-Making and Disagreement." *Social Forces,* 1957, *35,* 314–318.

Trist, E. "The Evolution of Socio-Technical Systems." Occasional paper, no. 2. Toronto, Canada: Quality of Working Life Centre, June 1981.

Tuckman, J., and Lorge, I. Individual Ability as a Determinant of Group Superiority. *Human Relations,* 1962, *15,* 45–51.

Turoff, M., and Hiltz, S. R. "International Potentials of Computerized Conferencing." In L. Parker and C. Olgren (eds.), *The Teleconferencing Resource Book.* New York: Elsevier Science, 1984.

Tyson, J. "Video Teleconferencing Cuts Costs, Boosts Productivity." *Management Review,* Jan. 1986, p. 5.

U.S. General Accounting Office. *Productivity Sharing Programs: Can They Contribute to Productivity?* Gaithersburg, Md.: U.S. General Accounting Office, Document Handling and Information Services Facility (AFMD-81-22), 1981.

Vallee, J. "The Network Revolution: Promises and Pitfalls in the Use of Information Technology." In G. R. Geiss and N. Viswanathan (eds.), *The Human Edge.* New York: Haworth Press, 1986.

Van de Ven, A. H. "Group Decision Making and Effectiveness." In D. Robey and S. Altman (eds.), *Organization Development: Progress and Perspectives.* New York: Macmillan, 1982.

Van de Ven, A. H., and Delbecq, A. L. "Nominal Versus Interacting Group Process for Committee Decision-Making Effectiveness." *Academy of Management Journal,* 1971, *14,* 203–212.

"Videoconferencing: No Longer Just a Sideshow." *Business Week,* Nov. 12, 1984, pp. 116–120.

White, D. D., and Bednar, D. A. "Quality Circle Procedures and Problems: A Survey of U.S. Firms." In D. Ray (ed.), *Applying Systematic Knowledge to Problems of Organization and*

Management. State College: Southern Management Association, Mississippi State University, 1983.

White, J. K. "The Scanlon Plan: Causes and Correlates of Success." *Academy of Management Journal,* 1979, *22,* 292–312.

Witte, J. F. *Democracy, Authority, and Alienation in Work: Workers' Participation in an American Corporation.* Chicago: University of Chicago Press, 1980.

Index

193

first vote, 60–65; for a document
review meeting, 79–80; need for
permanent use of a secret ballot,
40–41; no optimal procedure for,
66; only INGT uses of decision
by majority vote, 55, 80; the
problem of preference gaps, 67–
68; ranking versus rating scales,
67–69; sample ballot, 63; sample
tally sheet, 64; second vote
procedure, 66; use of point assignment in, 69; use of SPAN III
(Social Participatory Allocative
Network) for, 69–70; value of the
second-vote option, 65–66
Vredenburgh, D. J., 2, 168, 181

Wakeley, J., 13, 184
Waterman, R. H., Jr., 104, 105, 126,
  189
White, D. D., 118, 191–192
White, J. K., 7, 192
White, P. N., 146, 181
White, T. H., 186
Williams, E., 146, 190
Wilpert, A., 190
Witte, J. F., 131, 192
Work redesign. *See* Job redesign
Workshops, teleconferencing, 142

Young, I., 147, 181–182